Walking with Eve in the Loved City

Miller Williams Poetry Series
EDITED BY BILLY COLLINS

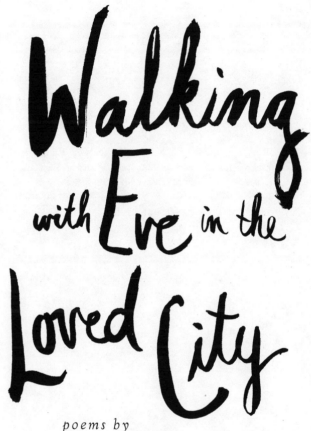

Walking with Eve in the Loved City

poems by
Roy Bentley

The University of Arkansas Press • Fayetteville • 2018

Copyright © 2018 by The University of Arkansas Press

All rights reserved
Manufactured in the United States of America

ISBN: 978-1-68226-057-9
eISBN: 978-1-61075-633-4

22   21   20   19   18   5   4   3   2   1

Designed by Liz Lester

⊗ The paper used in this publication meets the minimum
requirements of the American National Standard for Permanence
of Paper for Printed Library Materials Z39.48–1984

Library of Congress Control Number: 2017954147

SERIES EDITOR'S PREFACE

When the University of Arkansas Press asked if I would act as editor for the coming year's annual poetry prize named in honor of Miller Williams—the long-time director of the press and its poetry program—I was quick to accept. Since 1988 when he published my first full-length book, *The Apple That Astonished Paris*, I have felt indebted to Miller, who died in January 2015 at the age of eighty-four. From the beginning of his time at the press, it was Miller's practice to publish one poet's first book every year. Then in 1990 this commitment was formalized when Miller awarded the first Arkansas Poetry Prize. Fittingly, it was renamed the Miller Williams Poetry Prize after his retirement.

When Miller first spotted my poetry, I was forty-six years old with two chapbooks only. Not a pretty sight.

I have him to thank for first carrying me across that critical line dividing *no book* from *book*, thus turning me, at last, into a "published poet." I was especially eager to take on the task of selecting books (with the assistance of many invaluable screeners) for the Miller Williams Poetry Prize because it is a publication prize, which may bring to light other first books.

Miller Williams was more than my first editor. Over the years, he and I became friends, but even before my involvement with the press, he served as a kind of literary father to me. His straightforward, sometimes folksy, sometimes witty and always trenchant poems became to me models of how poems could sound and how they could go. He was one of the poets who showed me that humor could be a legitimate mode in poetry—that a poem could be humorous without being silly or merely comical. He also showed me that a plain-spoken poem did not have to be imaginatively plain. Younger poets today could learn much from his example, as I did.

Given his extensive and distinguished career, it's surprising that Miller didn't enjoy a more prominent position on the

American literary map. As his daughter became well-known as a singer and recording artist, Miller became known to many as the father of Lucinda Williams. Miller and Lucinda even appeared on stage together several times performing a father-daughter act of song and poetry. And Miller enjoyed a bright, shining moment when Bill Clinton chose him to be the inaugural poet at his second inauguration in 1997. The poem he wrote for that day, "Of History and Hope," is a meditation on how "we have memorized America." In turning to the children of our country he broadens a nursery rhyme question by asking "How does our garden grow?" Occasional poems, especially for occasions of such importance, are notoriously difficult—some would say impossible—to write with success. But Miller rose to this lofty occasion and produced a winner. His confident reading of the poem before the nation added cultural and emotional weight to the morning's ceremony.

Apart from such public recognitions, most would agree that Miller's fuller legacy lies in his teaching and publishing career, which covered four decades. In that time, he published over a dozen books of his own poetry and literary theory. His literary work as poet and editor is what will speak for Miller in the years to come. The qualities of his poems make them immediately likeable and pleasurable. They sound as if they were spoken, not just written, and they show a courteous, engaging awareness of the presence of a reader. Miller knew that the idea behind a good poem is to make the reader feel something, rather than to merely display the poet's emotional state, which usually boils down to some form of misery. Miller also possessed the authority of experience to produce poems that were just plain wise.

With these attributes in mind, I began the judging of this year's prize. On the lookout for poems that Miller would approve of, that is, poems that seemed to be consciously or unconsciously in the Miller Williams School, I read and read. But in reading these scores of manuscripts, I realized that applying such narrow criteria would be selling Miller short. His tastes in poetry were clearly broader than the stylistic territory of his own verse; he published poets as different from one another as John Ciardi and Jimmy Carter. I readjusted and began to look for poems I thought Miller would delight in reading, instead of echoes of his own poems. Broadening the field of judgment brought happy results. It took some second-guessing, but I'm confident that Miller would enthusiastically approve of this year's selections. The work of three very different poets, who have readability, freshness of language, and seriousness of intent in common, stood out from the stack of submissions.

Roy Bentley is a child of the movies. In one of the poems in *Walking with Eve in the Loved City*, this self-described "fat-kid eighth grader" is watching *Bullitt* for the third time straight while an impartial usher looks on. The distance between this Ohio boy stuffing himself with popcorn and Steve McQueen gunning his Mustang GT 390 collapses as the poem rises to an ecstatic celebration of "a communion of terrific car chases wherein thunderous / algorithms of horsepower rule." In another poem, the hormonal uptick of adolescence caused by attending "Sex Ed classes / with our dads" is registered while the speaker watches *Son of Frankenstein* in his "pj's at Gary Laberman's house on Comanche Drive." When he and his friends become sexually active, the poet is certain, "townspeople will start lighting torches." These poems get where they're going by way of long, loopy sentences dotted with references to high and low culture. Helpfully, Bentley is fond of titles that inform and orient the reader rather than obstruct entry to the poem. I appreciated "Saturday Afternoon at the Midland Theatre in Newark, Ohio" almost as much as I did "Ringo Starr Answers Questions on *Larry King Live* about the Death of George Harrison." And poems about Rimbaud and Robert E. Lee anchor us in history then set us adrift in the poet's revisionist take on these glorified figures. This is a lively collection that instructs, delights, and uplifts.

When asked how to account for the distinctive guitar work of the Rolling Stones, Ron Wood said, "I think it's a bit like the ancient art of weaving." This is a skill that Scott Cunningham knows well (and even acknowledges in an epigraph), for several of his poems make a variety of designs by braiding together strands of their own lines. In one poem titled "Fugue 52" (implying there are more to come), and in another, a sonnet sequence titled "Now a Word about Twentieth-Century Music," repeated lines are used as threads and connective tissue to hold the poems in tight order. That Morton Feldman, the composer, makes Zelig-like appearances in both of these poems should come as no coincidence because the poems themselves exhibit a musical structure, though thankfully not as complexly experimental as that of a Feldman composition. The collection, *Ya Te Veo,* offers many other delights including a wiggy explanation of how the New York School was formed and an updated, parodic version of "Dover Beach" that comes out of the box with "The sea is a bomb tonight." Also notable is a poem about a victim of the Salem witch trials, Giles Corey, who was put to death by a now mercifully shelved method called "pressing," in which the victim lies under a board, which is then loaded with heavier and heavier stones until a confession or death is achieved. "More weight," Corey memorably demands from his executioners. And don't miss "Poems about Concentration for People Who Can't Concentrate," perhaps a distant cousin of Geoff Dyer's essay collection *Yoga for People Who Can't be Bothered to Do It.* A sample: "You're at your desk. / You can't concentrate. / Imagine if not concentrating / was concentrating." In sum, a distinctive collection by a very savvy poet.

What often lures us into poems and keeps our interest is the poet's sensibility, that intangible element that arises from a poet's tone, his or her verbal personality. That is what hooked me when I began to read *Narcissus Americana.* Travis Mossotti's tone is a mixture of irony and true feeling, or rather a balancing act between the cool of one and the warmth of the other. Here's a poet who laments the absence of poets getting drunk in their poems, "like William Matthews did." A smart, informed melancholia can be found in many of these poems, including an exclamatory ode to condoms that is peppered with Shelley-like Os, and a poem detailing an encounter at a concert with a woman whose life and body are ruined by meth—a poem that ends surprisingly with the ceiling of the famous chapel whose name rhymes with hers: *Christine*. I trust this poet who can tell the tenor from the vehicle and whose poem "Cigar" shows us that many times a cigar is not just a cigar. Mossotti can also produce a narrative adventure, as he does in "Abandoned Quarry," where diving underwater at night conveys a cinematic level of excitement and tension. Producing poems that are clear and mysterious, funny and serious, Travis Mossotti is one of a thriving group of American poets writing these days whose work exposes the mendacity of those who cite "difficulty" as an excuse for not reading poetry.

In short, we have here a gathering of poets whose work, I think, would have fully engaged and gladdened Miller Williams. Because I have sat with him there, I can picture Miller in his study turning these pages, maybe stopping to make a pencil note in a margin. Miller's hope, of course, was that the poems published in this series would find a broad readership, ready to be delighted and inspired. I join my old friend and editor in that wish.

Billy Collins

ACKNOWLEDGMENTS

Many thanks to the editors of the journals and publications where these poems have previously appeared: *The 3288 Review,* "Nosferatu Exits the Garden State Parkway to Gas Up at the Wawa in Barnegat"; *2River,* "Astonished Man" (previously titled "The Death of Chance Locke"); *Able Muse,* "1975"; *The American Journal of Poetry,* "Jim Morrison & The Doors in Miami, 1969," "White Cane Lying in the Gutter in the Lane"; *Appalachian Heritage,* "Black Radio"; *The Atticus Review,* "Robert Plant Holding a Dove that Flew into His Hands, circa 1973," "Dressing after Sex"; *The Baltimore Review,* "One Wench in the House between Them," "O, Kindergarten"; *Bayou Magazine,* "The Nascent Soul Selects a Set of Appalachian Parents"; *Big Muddy, A Journal of the Mississippi River Valley,* "Live Nudes"; *Blackbird,* "Death at the Lakeshore"; *Bluestem,* "And the Blood Came Trickling Down"; *Chicago Quarterly Review,* "Byron and Shelley, Maintaining," "Beautiful Ohio"; *The Chiron Review,* "Jeff Goldblum in *The Fly*"; *The Citron Review,* "Lee in the Orchard, 1865"; *Cleaver Magazine,* "The Color Yellow, Love, the Fall of Leaves in Autumn"; *Cream City Review,* "G"; *december,* "And the World All Leaves and Morning Air"; *Evening Street Review,* "God Shows Up in Iowa"; *Fifth Wednesday Journal,* "Einstein and Chaplin at the Movies"; *Florida English,* "The Dark Knight, On His Day Off"; *The Florida Review,* "Watching the Night Approach of Tropical Storm Rita," "The Fury of a Patient Man"; *Free State Review,* "God's Circus at Its Wintering Grounds in Florida," "When Billie Holiday Sings about Southern Trees"; *JMWW,* "The Pop-up Book of Falling in Love," "Truck Picture, 1962," "Herons, in April in Ohio," "With the Lights of Houses Flashing By in the Darkness"; *The Journal,* "You Must Drive This Car"; *The Louisville Review,* "Whatever Else, This Memory Resembles a Dance"; *Magnolia,* "The Last Man on Earth Takes a Walk in Jupiter, Florida," "Dixie Highway"; *The Main Street Rag,* "The Lives of My Poems after I'm Gone"; *Moon City Review,* "WD8RBB"; *North American Review,*

"Puberty"; *nthposition,* "Can't Help Falling in Love"; *New Works Review,* "Leaving the Regal Jupiter 18 Cinema Singing . . ."; *Off the Coast,* "American Christian," "The Mountain Elvises Get Ready for Talent Night"; *One,* "Transcendence"; *Orange Coast Review,* "A Palestinian Boy Looks through the Rubble inside His Home in a Refugee Camp near Tyre," "Jack Johnson Returns to His America to Eat Cold Eels and Think Distant Thoughts"; *Poydras Review,* At the Wheel of the *Pilar,* Ernest Hemingway Addresses the Breezes off the Coast of Cuba; *Rappahannock Review,* "How Not to Spell *Gymnasium*"; *Rattle,* "Ringo Starr Answers Questions on *Larry King Live* about the Death of George Harrison"; *Shenandoah,* "Nosferatu in Florida"; *Soundings Review,* "25 Astonishing Things to Do with a Pocket Handkerchief," "Our Local Heavens"; *Southern Ohio Anthology,* "Far"; *The Southern Review,* "Saturday Afternoon at the Midland Theatre in Newark, Ohio"; *Spoon River Poetry Review,* "Hellhound"; *Steinbeck Now,* "James Dean Kissing Julie Harris in *East of Eden,*" "Fitzgerald and Zelda, February, 1921"; *Tampa Review,* "Unicyclist with UM Umbrella"; *Tar River Poetry,* "Mexican Clowns Deny Costume Killer of Drug Trafficking Boss Belonged to Their Profession," "The Days of Miracle and Wonder"; *Texas Review,* "The Silence of the Belt When It Is Not Striking the Child"; *The Tishman Review,* "Walking with Eve in the Loved City"; *UCity Review,* "The Force of Right Words," "Night Migration"; *Valparaiso Poetry Review,* "My Father's Love Letters," "Rimbaud Dying"; *What Rough Beast,* "America as Ex."

I'm grateful to the National Endowment for the Arts, the Ohio Arts Council, and the Florida Division of Cultural Affairs. Also, to Okla Elliott and Hannah Stephenson for including "Saturday Afternoon at the Midland Theatre in Newark, Ohio" in New Poetry from the Midwest 2014 (Milwaukee, WI/Urbana, IL: New American Press, 2015). *Mudlark: An Electronic Journal of Poetry & Poetics* published a chapbook called "Saturday Afternoon at the Midland Theatre in Newark, Ohio" drawn from the pages of this collection.

This book is for Sherry Bentley.

CONTENTS

2

3

4

1

We have two lives. The life we learn with and the life we live with after that.

—Iris Lemon in *The Natural*
(BERNARD MALAMUD)

Robert Plant Holding a Dove
that Flew into His Hands, circa 1973

—photograph from the concert at Kezar Stadium
in San Francisco: June 2, 1973

The wing-flutter resolves like a breath of fog
by San Francisco Bay. Like sand or white sails.
This year, every snapshot of Robert Plant onstage
describes the outline and contour of his cock
through jeans. This is that. But the heart inside
the successful crooner is what it is: Frank Sinatra
with a smidgen of Elvis tossed in for good measure:

Shelley's Adonais resurrected with a mane of hair
and management, a record deal and Jimmy Page.
Now the fingers tipped with nicotine gesture
to the starveling crowd about to feast—
the hand dealing with both a lit Marlboro
and a bottle of English beer. Which is when
the rock dove lands on the other hand. Settles

like news of the death of Keats settled on Shelley.
This congregation still wants directions to Paradise
if not ushered to the stairs. Taught the shibboleth
for entry. What it gets is the flight of the dove,
impromptu cooing, the talons ringing fingers
as if what we call beautiful is straightening
the curve of its spine and starting to sing.

Our Local Heavens

Roy the Father hands Roy the Son the Testor's glue.
Says, *go easy* as he soliloquizes about the engine,
saying that the 265-horsepower unsupercharged dual-
overhead-cam four-valves-per-cylinder automobile
was the most expensive, most powerful straight-eight
built in Des Moines, Iowa or anywhere in those days.
Roy the Father tosses out *built entirely by hand*,
which is printed on the Monogram box. He shows
how 1/32nd scale pieces dry-fit. Says the Model J
is like a Duesy—the movie version Daisy Buchanan
raced over Myrtle Wilson with in *The Great Gatsby*.
Roy the Son doesn't know then that Roy the Father
has the date of the novel wrong, the model mixed up.
Roy the Son is inventing scenarios whereby the vehicle
raises rooster tails of red dirt, a captain of industry or king
or Hollywood film star at the wheel and driving far too fast.
Which is how building the Duesenberg ends—the model
doused and set alight, its chimeric canary-gold plastic melting,
Roy the Father having exited Roy the Son's life, a son's stock
of enchanted objects decreased, the count diminished by one,
as Gatsby's was after the green light on Daisy's dock dimmed.
Tonight, the local heavens of the room smell of Testor's glue.
Roy the Son is still a boy and still nuts about Roy the Father.
The tricky cement is hardening as it should. Not too quickly
since model building is the chance for a father to tell a story
whose end isn't predicated on a knowledge of good and evil
or understanding what fathers owe sons without knowing it.
Disaster is everywhere. Yet, for now, most of that is outside.
In here, chrome-trimmed running boards reflect dreamlight.
Roy the Son grasps the Duesy and makes a flying motion.

How Not to Spell *Gymnasium*

for Al Maginnes

As for the rest, they spat consonants and vowels
in correct order while I was in the john
and so not around when the Bs were called,
my phonological bowels a reproach to thoughts
of metalinguistic glory. I wanted an easy one:
Diarrhea: d-i-a-r-r-h-e-a. Diarrhea.
Like all of my life to come, I wanted
what I wanted and got what I was handed
instead. Most children like language—
they breathe near painful meaning, kids,
and they look you dead in the eyes
until they forget—as I did—or look away
and dash to error. Shame. For the rest
of my life, I'd recall what being in a hurry
gets you: asked to have a seat at a desk
of carved-and-initialed mutable moments.
All right, so I spat a *j* first fucking thing
and had to playact at being glad for others
while being taught a valuable lesson: not
to be looking at Shelley Staddon's budding
breasts; as if I could stop myself, as if, like Jesus
who, on the cross, learned about phonemes
blending and segmenting—what's the Aramaic
for *sacrifice*—and that loss decants too easily
from us, like Jesus, like that *j* instead of *g*,
spewed while thinking of acrobatic *c-l-o-u-d-s*
above the gray-shiny slide and a Jungle Jim—

there was that resurrectionist of a *j*, which
had tricked me into thinking there is no trick,
that once you understand the future has breasts—
Breasts: b-r-e-a-s-t-s—you watch your step down
from Rolling Fields Elementary School's stage
past what is beyond words, thinking you know
a way to move through the life you're given.

1975

Once upon a time you dressed so fine
You threw the bums a dime in your prime, didn't you?
　　　　—BOB DYLAN, "Like a Rolling Stone"

My girlfriend Sherry asks why Lindsey Buckingham
is so thin as she cradles the album *Buckingham Nicks*.
This is before he and Stevie Nicks join Fleetwood Mac.
I tell her he's a rock star and that rock stars are ghosts.
A turntable spins. The small apartment smells of sex,
marijuana. Most of one wall is an *Easy Rider* poster.
Fonda and Hopper on Harley choppers. In a corner
of the poster, a *Discover America* sticker.

Saigon is falling. Sherry shows me a *Newsweek*—
pages of color photographs of helicopters, sailors
shoving them from the deck of the *USS Okinawa*
into the South China Sea, chopper blades nicking
the rough waters of the Pacific, spinning to a stop
on a turntable-axis of collective national disgrace.
She points to the regimental insignia and US flag.
I rise and stagger to the turntable. Lift the needle.

I know what she wants: any album by Bob Dylan
where two lovers are the A-plus-B in a mathematics
of fulfillment-for-a-little-while, that equation solved
though the republics of the sad earth slide into collapse,
ruin, refugees crowding onto last ships where the deck air
reeks of diesel and human sweat and a blue transistor radio
blares: *I see your hair is burnin' / Hills are filled with fire*
If they say I never loved you / You know they are a liar.

Walking with Eve in the Loved City

1. *John and George Wore Matching Black Swim Trunks*

*We settled in the Key Wester hotel. For a few hours,
on September 10th, the boys relaxed. John waded
into a swimming pool with several members of the
Exciters, a '60s pop group—3 girls, 1 guy, all African
American. The pictures of John in the pool with
black women enraged Southern reporters. The pho-
tos became an overnight sensation.*

—LARRY KANE

This is 1964. After a photo shoot for *Life* magazine
where three black women lounge in a swimming pool
at the Key Wester with John Lennon. At poolside,
they aren't raising their middle finger to the South.
They don't see it that way. They're negotiating,
by phone, the segregated seating at the Gator Bowl.
They won't perform. Meaning there is right and fair
and this isn't that. George Paul Ringo kid reporters.
They're doing what good lads have always done: Talk

women. And no one wants Lennon interviewed. No one
wants a bloody scuffle like at the clubs in Hamburg. They
want Johnny writing hit songs to *buy* hotel swimming pools.
They blame scheduling. And the hurricane. And then perform,
the show like thread leading back to the matching swim trunks.
Across Florida, in St. Augustine, a white motel owner-operator
splashes muriatic acid into a pool where blacks are swimming.
The photograph makes Jimmy Brock as notable as the Beatles
in water where the past is light and drags everything with it.

2. *How Barbie and Ken Wound Up on* The Daily Show *with* Jon Stewart

If Barbie is so popular, why do you have to buy her friends?
—STEVEN WRIGHT

Bored with being dolls, they wanted to give breath
and flesh to approximate lusts. Give motion a try.
When the laptop screensaver was the only light,
they sloughed the definitions of non-existence.
Ken made a move and Barbie answered, stroking
his Interesting Place with its suggestion of genitalia.
She had absolutely no idea there were others watching.
Still, she wasn't unhappy when it wound up on YouTube.
They didn't intend to upstage Arnold Schwarzenegger or

Congressman Weiner or that IMF banker who'd assaulted
hotel maids when he wasn't working to loot the free world.
They didn't see themselves as circus freaks, Ken and Barbie,
but there was the matter of fame. And what *is* an icon to do?
Of course Stewart's people broke out dollhouse patio furniture,
as if the only response to Barbara Millicent Roberts and cohort
was walk-on music by The Beach Boys and spinning vortices
of red and white and blue. Stewart: *Do comparisons between
dollhood and Frankenstein's monster ever bother you two?*

3. Walking with Eve in the Loved City

And the loved city? Only at a distance can it be loved.
—MARK JARMAN

Since all things are present at the same time in one place,
and since that place has a name we translate as "paradise,"
she dangled before me in a first-language of crucifixes.
Her eyes appraised me like a sale rack. The look said
that it would be getting dark forever somewhere soon.
I figured she had the keys to the kingdom or a Bentley
parked like a prophecy up the road in the moonlight.
Clearly, she was unhappy. I guessed Adam was off
inventing parimutuel off-track betting or the trifecta.

There were angels. Some with red-white-and-blue wings.
And Eve asked me if a black angel was subject to searches
that a white angel wasn't. I reminded her where we were.
I didn't want to get tagged for staring—she was a knock-out—
and so I looked off at a robed man who was bending low
to talk Pashto to a predator part lion part Nile crocodile.
I'm not afraid of this thing, he said, straightening up.
He reached to pet the lion-croc. Turned. Stared at me.
Then: *I'm more afraid of Americans, aren't you?*

Jeff Goldblum in *The Fly*

When he gets Geena Davis into his laboratory,
she winds up taking off a black silk stocking.
A reporter, there for the story, she rolls the
stocking down her thigh then knee then calf,
as if the mixing of business and pleasure goes
with the territory. Something she knows about.
She steps out of her stocking. Hands it to him,
smiling. And he dissolves and rematerializes it.

White people shouldn't mix with black silk stockings,
or mix them with science. They can't handle it. Cut
to her taking the story to her editor who calls Jeff
Goldblum/Seth Brundle a con man. A magician.
Cut to the lab: a baboon in a telepod, the animal
zapped to become—yuk!—a squirming mass.
Red-goo monkey steak but alive and in pain.

Seth then pontificates about the poetry of flesh.
He says the computer translates or mistranslates
what it supposes flesh to be. Says the problem
is the computer can only repeat an impression
of a baboon. Which is his and isn't even close.
No understanding of poetry yields no monkey
reassembled in approximately correct fashion.

They kiss—she kisses him—they fall together.
After a breakthrough revelation about the body,
a next baboon bounds out intact. Monkey see,

monkey do: Seth goes next, the stowaway fly
on the window of the teleporter his undoing.
What is science if not poetry translated? Of
course the experiment turns to shit. (It's love,
why wouldn't it?) Seth starts to crave sugar
and fuck like Superman on steroids. Lectures
about wanting to *really* penetrate the flesh.

He's buzzing now. To think, it all started
with the best intentions. And love, which
we hope will absolve us of everything.

Fitzgerald and Zelda, February 1921

All good writing is swimming under water and holding your breath.

—F. SCOTT FITZGERALD

In the photograph, Zelda wears a fur and hat.
Scott has on a top coat and gloves. It's winter.
He said Zelda had *an eternally kissable mouth*.
Said that he loved stories of her in Montgomery.
He'd begin: *Montgomery had telephones in 1910.*
It's April. A warm day. Magnolias are blooming.
Zelda—ten years old—has rung up the operator

to dispatch the fire department. She climbs out
onto a roof to wait rescue. Lots of white blossoms
are falling on small shoulders. Landing in her hair.
She's sitting, smoothing her dress when they come.
Whatever else, they looked swell in photographs.
He'd say, *Zelda drew flyers from Camp Sheridan*
who did figure eights over her Montgomery home.

They crashed their biplanes trying to impress her.
What he would never say: *Then she married me.*
As if what happened to her later was his fault
or a series of regrets for which he was to blame.
In 1921, each existed to watch the other move—

This Side of Paradise was a hit, he was soaring.
Zelda wanted to soar herself. Float like a ballerina.

At the end of the day she wanted what she wanted:
a ticket out of Alabama. Excitement. Breathlessness.
After her third breakdown, the years in sanatoriums,
visitors whispered, *She was a beauty once.* Trapped
at last in a burning asylum, the fire real, Zelda Sayre
Fitzgerald died locked in. Screaming to be rescued.
He would've been dead, buried, for years by then.

Saturday Afternoon at the Midland Theatre in Newark, Ohio

Slouched in a theater seat and watching *Bullitt* for the third
time, a look I get from an usher might best be described
as granting a general amnesty and full pardon for my
having shelled out only the one admission price. There's
the balcony with its blue and red curved seat backs. By a
door to the upstairs men's room a framed likeness of the
Civil War drummer boy, Johnny Clem, whose baby-faced
looks and sudden-dark hair remind me of a young Italian,
then Sal Mineo in *Rebel Without a Cause*. There's that
angels-in-the-architecture grand gesture of a ceiling, the
wall of drapes, eloquently pleated purple. And there's the
screen framed in its filigree of gold and silver. The usher
is accommodating me by simply not noticing—I'm on my
third popcorn, third enormous Coca-Cola, second box of
Milk Duds, when I realize I'm happy. Elated. In Ohio at
fourteen you're disappointed most of the time. So I want
to tell Frank Bullitt just how it feels to be from Dayton and
new here, a fat-kid eighth grader at Fulton Middle School.
But then, Steve McQueen is French-kissing Jacqueline
Bisset good morning. Strapping on a shoulder holster
and .38 pistol. Now he's stopped at the corner of Clay and
Taylor, searching the pockets of his trench coat/suit coat
for change. I've loved that look all afternoon. The usher
reacts as if that says it, that fuck-the-world expression of
Frank Bullitt as he gives up and bangs the cover and steals

a newspaper. Turns out, 1968 isn't for the faint of heart.
You need a Mustang GT 390. Ice water for a blood type.
A tolerance for the visages of the dead you made dead,
slaughtering out of that old American purity of motive that
dissolves into a communion of terrific car chases wherein
thunderous algorithms of horsepower rule.

Whatever Else, This Memory
Resembles a Dance

My earliest recollection of my grandmother Potter involves a warning.
It was about certain terpsichorean behavior: *No Dancing on the Sabbath.*
This would've been before we moved to the brick house in Kettering.
I only know it stuck and became *that which is older than memory,*
a word-for-word Eleventh Commandment she authored then forgot.
It was as if we were together in a house of ten thousand candles,
she and I, and she'd issued an exhortation to steer clear of matches,
then was jolted by a love of fire and brightness. Maybe I made it up.
Either way, I'd say to her, *Granny, remember when I was a small boy*

and you told me never to dance on Sundays? She'd say, *No, Roy,*
I don't remember that. If forgetting is older than history, older than
original sin, then so is making shit up. Meaning, I can't say for sure.
Maybe a doctrine against dance never actually issued from her mouth,
though it's exactly the kind of directive she was inclined to spew forth.
My mother challenges a memory I have of Sonny and Bobby Osborne
playing music in our house on Comanche. In those days, she worked
with the guitar player's girlfriend May. May lived with us in the house
on that low hill. My parents had just divorced, and Benny Birchfield

had dragged the bluegrass duo from Kentucky to Ohio. I remember
Granny coming out of her bedroom in a housecoat. She was in a huff.
I recall her telling them *Quiet down!* and hearing *Sorry, Miss Potter.*
But if Groucho Marx didn't have a duck that dropped from the ceiling
with the secret word, then I didn't hear a prohibition against Sabbath

dancing and the Osborne Brothers and Benny Birchfield never played in our kitchen, my granny waiting in the anarchy of light at the edges of seeing, standing like God (no fan of banjo and Appalachian fiddle) or Moses in the doorway. About to call it a night and throw them out.

The Silence of the Belt
When It Is Not Striking the Child

—Billy Collins, "Silence"

I had been laughing at my mother, and she did not like
being laughed at, especially by a son who saw his father
stealing the plates from her Olds on his way out the door
as cause for sniggering. The problem was, I couldn't stop.
Tides of out-of-body delight kept bubbling up. Breaking.
Until she left the room. Returned having rescued a belt
he had abandoned in his rush to be done with us.
We were in the kitchen. And I remember backing up
to the refrigerator. Begging for mercy. Forgiveness.
Her voice rose and fell as she tracked me to strike.
My legs-arms-back burned. The palm of one hand.
I had never been so utterly shamed. So humiliated.
I'd pissed myself, I saw after as she jerked me up
from a black tile floor saying, *Laugh some more.*

Maybe I have no call to show her in that light.
We had a lithograph of *The Blue Boy* on a wall.
The den had a gray sectional sofa. A color TV.
In the kitchen cabinet were Oreos. Pop-Tarts.
Outside, an Olds that wasn't going anywhere.
Don't act as if you haven't seen such houses.
Haven't lived on an analogous street where
mothers enacted similar torments. Fifty years
have ticked by. And I recall sliding down

the side of our Westinghouse refrigerator,
a boy-cheek compelled to the cool metal
as I asked to be permitted to live a while.
How could I know she wouldn't kill me?
Hadn't I just witnessed the end of love?

Can't Help Falling in Love

We're parked under luminous eaves of aluminum
& it's a summer night & the driver's side window
is rolled down on my father's '57 Ford Ranchero.
The carhop has brought us hamburgers & Cokes
& rested a tray under a Seeburg speaker playing
an Elvis Presley song. The carhop hangs around
like she can't imagine (or doesn't care) my father
is married. Sure enough, he leans out to touch her
on the arm & hand. A nametag reads *Georgia*.

Georgia the Carhop looks a lot like my mother
if my mother were a waitress at the Parkmoor
on Woodman Drive & had movie-star breasts
& piled-up Dolly Parton ringlets & a uniform
that is itself a way of speaking. She leans down,
says something & Ohio is a little more like heaven.

Miss Rocket Tits is talking through the window.
I answer her between bites of my cheeseburger
& a choking swallow of soft drink. I tell her
my name & that it's the same as his—*Roy*—
& she laughs like she's been told (& knows)
a wonderful secret. She asks how old I am
& I have to think & not look at all (I'll stare)
at her bending over in her uniform. Her eyes
sparkle & one of my molded plastic army men

digs into me from a place in my pants pocket.
I feel my heart beat & beat like the telltale one
under the floor in the Poe story I've already read
& had nightmares about. I say *eight* & Georgia
smiles, leaves us the check & a wink my father
has to see (but maybe he doesn't), reaching out
into a night stamping its features on the blank
of our lives, his face a template for everything
that shines like Elvis Presley's movie-star hair,
the chrome on a waxed-to-perfection Ford truck.

The Force of Right Words

You could say the lie was a story about what didn't happen.
Not the tale of my falling and snapping the plastic stock
of a friend's Christmas-gift toy rifle. I told it,
the stretcher, to his mother. And didn't hesitate,
having schooled Wes, the friend, to nod and say nothing.
She had questions. And her line of interrogation was laced
with threat. The Cuban missile crisis had shaken us that year.
Kids had developed the habit of looking skyward in dread
and anticipation much of the time they played outdoors.
I saw that sky in the look on the face of Bernie Vines,
Wes' mother. The light of all-things-American, too.
Some are born to lying. I was a natural—angel-faced,
a few whisper-touch brushstrokes of frightened boy—
the sort of kid aware which details work. In what order.
Shared truth does exist, I discovered, but is contingent
upon its utterance not sounding like a scratched LP,
not repeating what the hearer expects to glide through.
It seems a lie can clear the air of a quantity of truth
after which a friend's trusting mother will accept
the hypothetical presence of rowdy older boys,
lanky representatives of the likely and possible
descended out of nowhere like crows to carrion.
Marauders from elsewhere. Adolescent thugs
coveting a replica-by-Mattel Winchester rifle.
Bernie bought my story until she got Wes alone.
When she stormed across a shared side yard

to enlighten my mother, she wasn't smiling.
But then she was. Bernie Vines was a nurse.
A veteran of the day-to-day and hour-to-hour
earthly realities of what's true most of the time,
minus the fine gold pixie dust we toss about for luck.
But I'd somehow shown that her austere morality
and principled moment can extend outward as it
bends. Like a length of plastic before it snaps.
The smile was that part of a clear blue Ohio sky
unfilled by doom, untrafficked yet by missiles.

Twenty-Five Astonishing Things to Do
with a Pocket Handkerchief

In the movie house of my mind I am Houdini
as an adolescent of twelve, practicing to be a magician.
I'm not yet Harry Houdini. I'm still Ehrich Weiss.
I hear Mother chattering to herself in Hungarian
in the kitchen of our house. I'm the Jewish boy
in a dark blue corduroy suit twilled with an exotic
other-fabric or felt as patch for the elbows. Both

my lace-up boots are stuffed with newspaper to fit.
A scarecrow-like reflection in a polished tabletop,
I'm as far as number twenty-four on my list of things
to accomplish with ordinary pocket handkerchiefs;
things like making a blond, blue-eyed neighbor girl
named Cecilia applaud the disappearance of an egg.
Cecilia flutters her frilly dress in the willow shade.

I check to be sure Mother isn't finished baking or
hasn't discovered, too late, I'm in my good clothes.
The facts of life as heady as bread-scent in the air,
I look to my audience of one. I'll need a big finish.
I step toward her as if she were the future, saying,
Abracadabra—. Cecilia smiles like this is money
in the First National Bank of Milwaukee, what

I'm about to conjure. Cecilia wants what I want.
She couldn't care less that I've a train to catch—

I'm planning to hop a freight and join the circus.
She leans to me as I wave open the square of silk
and hold it over our heads, saying whatever passes
for an incantation. We kiss, the noun *handkerchief*
forever-password for first love. Number twenty-five.

Ringo Starr Answers Questions on *Larry King Live* about the Death of George Harrison

First, Larry King mistakenly calls Ringo
George then asks him whether his passing,
George's, was expected. He answers that it was.
Says they knew he was sick. Had lung cancer.
I'm watching, though it's none of my business
how grief-stricken Ringo Starr was and likely
still is or whether he was there at the bedside
at the moment George left his life for some other,
if you can believe what George believed, which
was that we keep coming back till we get it right.
And when Ringo is about to let down his guard
and be a bit more self-disclosing, even honest,
Larry interrupts, asking, *Do you ever want to
pinch yourself?* And Ringo Starr says, *Sure.*
In 1988, years before, in another interview,
with George, years after Lennon's death,
Ringo confessed that he was the poorest Beatle
then laughed and blew cigarette smoke upward.
Which must've seemed terribly funny to George,
an inside joke, because he said *Hello, John* to
the smoke like it was Lennon (by virtue of his
acknowledged wealth) or some spirit he used to
conquer worlds with. Ringo says he was shocked
upon hearing the news of John Lennon's death,
but that George's was another thing entirely.
He doesn't quote from the Bhagavad Gita, but it's
as if he wants to say we continue on, are these *spirits*—

a sort of outrageous bliss even to think it, dumb luck
on the order of being hired as the Beatles' drummer.
Maybe he would have said it, with respect to George,
or ventured his own beliefs, if Larry hadn't butted in
to ask him which of the Beatles was the best musician.
You mean, now? And I want to laugh now because
maybe Ringo's imagining how hard it is to move
your hands after you're dead, or to move at all,
and how impossible it must be to keep time
and tempo in all that anonymous blankness,
the dark become your most imploring fan.

The Dark Knight, On His Day Off

As Bruce Wayne, he's practicing kicks in the backyard.
Blue-black shadows fall on an oak he batters to let it out—
all that fury and frustration at being so unsuper and a hero.

He's mindful there are paparazzi everywhere with cameras.
Eavesdropping on him. Spying. But he needs not to feel this.
Like he might want to take a life with one blow. Champions

don't behave like that. They kick old oaks until they're sore.
Maintaining the opinion others are worthy—that's the trick.
He recalls first battles. Against teens, really. Besting them

on a fire escape. Having to worry and catch an offender
as he went over. Ordering himself to reach for an ankle
and hold on. Which he did, lowering the sniveling kid

with a gentleness and concern the world shows no one.
He remembers the wrath of bystanders, and answering.
Seventy-eight acts of assault in the first five weeks. No

wonder the citizenry was slow to warm to his methods.
Schooled in morality and machine-gun fire, the noise
fists make stopping an aggressor in stride. So what

if he exists, in no small measure, because he's rich.
Rich guys with a conscience just kick ass differently.
An iPhone ringtone—"The William Tell Overture"—

says Alfred has prepared dinner. One final roundhouse
before toweling off. Ah, the effort this is! Ah, the hours
needed to win (then win again) the designation *Good*!

He heads in the direction of a door. Wayne Manor.
Sure, he's exhausted. Ready for a meal. A movie:
a. young Marlon Brando standing up to a beating.

Hellhound

This one lazes about by outcroppings, sniffing
itself as if it could smell anything but brimstone,
heady drifts of sulphur riding the indifferent day.
An unsolicitous look says the Almighty's minions
can go to—never mind. They say he chased cars
and caught one. No beast this definitively ugly
is also stupid, just distracted by the steady influx.

If there were double-wide trailers on the hillsides,
the hillsides awash in the trash of lives, and one
really big billboard for used clothing and maybe
a Nissan Ford Toyota Chrysler Chevy on blocks
in a sideyard, you'd swear you were home. Now
a priest bends to fluff a tuft of fur, jumps back
as if bitten. He crosses himself for the reason

that habits are what he has. The dog isn't buying
genuflection, the kindness. And it lunges at him,
at the hem of his cassock, trying to make a meal
of a being who reads Scripture in a sky's looting
light from the sacristy of the rooms of afternoon.
The mutt's no fan of sacerdotalism. Priestcraft.
His job: to devour whatever sort of thief passes.

A kind of divine judgment is in the dog's chains.
If the escape of the priest is a function of grace,

dumb luck, it is also the case that the animal was
tending to a wound received from rough handling.
Which, without possibility of healing, had festered.
Broken open. And nagged like knowing, to the day,
some exact length of time that constitutes forever.

Transcendence

There is the human in the drop-winged angels in El Greco
and the ellipses of youth in a milkmaid's face in Vermeer.

There are the spaces between notes in certain guitar solos
by Carlos Santana or Django Reinhardt in which existence
is reconstituted as bliss—orchestrations of mercurial joy.

There is the locker-room smile on Mickey Mantle's face
in the '56–'57 season, the patter of a titan in the ascendant.

There is the talk of afterlife and deities, the sage expression
of Caucasian-Christ-in-the-lighted-frame on church walls
and in funeral homes where the newly grieving delight
at *heaven* showing up on the tongue like a eucharist.

And for the poets there is a blankness before words
to be risen above like Dorothy's tornadic, sepia Kansas
in *The Wizard of Oz*, the way a metaphor in some hands
protects and serves like a pair of regulation ruby slippers,
a humbug behind the curtain of the page the best in us.

Maybe the way a lover looked at you after sex,
in the last soulful glow of arousal and climax,
spoke of an escalator to the stars, the escalator
melting like clocks or that one drop of blood
from a cracked-and-hatching egg of a world
in those paintings by Salvador Dali. Maybe

the only rising we do is out of this body.

2

Warden: *The patient that came in
yesterday is having a fit.*

Van Helsing: *Which one?*

Warden: *The one that bit the cow.*

—from *Nosferatu the Vampyre* (1979)

Nosferatu in Florida

Maybe vampires hear an annunciatory trumpet solo.
Maybe they gather at the customary tourist traps
like a blanket of pink flamingos plating a lake
and lakeshore by the tens of thousands to drink.
The whole tacky blood circus is theme park stuff
and as Disneyesque as lifting the lid on a casket
to flit about sampling the inexhaustible offerings
of O positive like the Sunday brunch at IHOP.
But if you had a booming, amphitheatrical voice
and had been recently rescued from the grave—
if you wore the republic of the dark like a cape
at Halloween, all bets would be off by the signage
for Paradise Tire & Service, a neon green royal palm.
Bela Lugosi could materialize on a trailer park lawn
and the locals would miss it, though lap dogs howled
as kingdoms rose and fell. You could say a kingdom
of fangs glows and drips red by the broken temples
and wide, well-lit aisles of Best Buy and Walmart.
By the shadowed homeless holding up placards
hand-lettered in English, as if the kindhearted
of the nations of the world spoke one language
and could be counted on to forgive misspellings,
bad syntax that announces one life is never enough.
The resurrection of the body is tough everywhere.
In the Sunshine State, despite eons to shake off loss,
a body carries the added burden of perpetual labor
and cyclical, inescapable debt. The dead know this.

Unicyclist with UM Umbrella

Say you're driving, idling in rush hour traffic,
and the wind has just shared its best open secret.
Say you've come from signing divorce papers.
The palm fronds, streetside, sag as if burdened.

Someone is navigating between cars, busting ass
to get from point A to B in a hellish downpour.
His slaloming of the stopped lines, on a unicycle,
dismantles the distances in a whoosh of inches.

A rain-diamonded thoroughfare sings of his tire,
the rooster-tailing arc of spray from it. It seems
impossible that there could be anyone so at ease
with what it takes to just press on. Like a surfer

stepped from an ocean that radiates through him.
They say we're electrons. Particles, wavelengths.
Still, it takes a native Floridian to move like this
with a University of Miami parasol as accessory.

The Sound of a Midnight Train in Florida

A night without stars. The coastal highway
awash in a red light as after brushfires, and me
driving, drawn to the going as if it were a fire
set and burning inside as the night becomes
the voices of the singer on the car stereo and
a CSX train passing beyond, nearer the water.
The singer on the CD wants her dead friend,
a suicide, to acknowledge what he forfeited:
See what you lost when you left this world?
This sweet old world. What you lost when
you left this world, this sweet old world. . . .
The train noises are as plaintive as it gets.
And, sure, sweet. But something else—
a magnitude of longing as unbearable as
failed hopes in the wheel-rhythm rockings
of steel traveling at the speed of lonesome,
a melancholy long associated with trains
in much the same way we marry Florida to
sunshine and beaches. Truth is, the sun isn't
all it's cracked up to be; in fact, it's deadly,
or so my Norwegian dermatologist lectured
the last time she burned the umpteenth set
of precancerous basal cells from my face.
I've been running around in the light all day.
With the top still down on my Solara, feeling
a beer buzz the way some feel faith in God
or an afterlife-Heaven of Florida-sunny days,
wind in my hair like the fingers of some honey

with minty-fresh breath and a Bond girl body,
my red face the wages of days of good weather,
Lucinda Williams cranked *way* up, I'm flying
past lonesome all the way to the ocean. East.
Toward a break in the clouds showing stars,
the one heaven that, after death, will be there.

Watching the Night Approach
of Tropical Storm Rita

Moonlight, pewter-colored ocean, bougainvillea
and Jupiter Beach resolving into palm shadow,
low notes of wind and a thousand-handed slap
on the Atlantic's rolling plain of dark, our faces
the easy radiance at a double door to a lanai
where you released a cricket earlier that day.
A royal poinciana sways beyond pools of rain,

and our reflected twins in the hurricane glass
look back at us like a species of statue
vanishing and coming together again
at last in the soft vestments of clouds.
A scrim of the usual stars and planets
sparks like the eyes of feral animals
shifting shape in the sky above A1A.

Flapping red pennants on tall poles—
to warn swimmers, I'm told—say a cargo
of breezes from West Africa, Cape Verde,
has come ashore to tug at all things rooted,
just now, as a crazy few wade a path of water
and cricket song past walls of beach chairs
turning gold against the wild, bright waves.

The Last Man on Earth Takes a Walk in Jupiter, Florida

It would happen on a day like any other in South Florida,
the projector in a revival house movie theater looping
Treasure of the Sierra Madre or Errol Flynn in *Captain Blood*
because someone had hooked up a generator, pull-started it,
and finished off the last of the popcorn and Pepsi. Maybe
they'd buried the corpses or burned them and boarded up.
Maybe a tsunami of communicable disease had thinned
the unmanageable ranks over a period of years; a plague
that, in its final months, assumed withering proportions.
Nothing absurd about thinking of one freakish survivor
as the fly of hope not yet swatted dead. Maybe hostilities,
if it was a war, ran their course elsewhere, mercifully up-

or downwind, but the oceans died. Whatever happened,
we were warned that unintended consequences are a bitch.
Now, as if the soul were a set of casual clothing from the Gap
laid out for a final outing in rain or fabulous sun, he stoops
to dress. Returning to the world is a habit hard to break.
He readies himself to pass flood-deserted strip malls—
lines of solar-powered and pointless signage. This time,
he walks a service road to a park named for Burt Reynolds.
When he speaks, a voice knocks around in the seasonal
theater of the body. Resonates. Farther on, he glimpses
water finding track by the dead raised roots of date palms.
The snapping of a tarp on a dock nearby is benediction.

Bees

The guy originally from Chicago phones from the driveway
to say he's here to get rid of those black-bodied whirligigs
whose wings beat the air a gazillion times per second
in defiance of both the laws of aerodynamics and gravity.
South Florida's rife with tales of plunder and forfeiture,
and somehow the little air pirates insinuate themselves
into the eaves as a consequence of imperfect attention,
mine, but what do I care so long as they don't take over?

I'm one man, out of place before a backdrop of flowers
and honey-colored beaches, who has nowhere else to go.
Nothing but respect for the industriousness of insects
making an inventory of the rooflines of communities
with place names reflecting the guilty weave of history
and hope that never stops being its own undertow.
In fact, I wish my words worked like carpenter bees,
first light to dusk, answering a clear morning of need

to make the unruly world over just so and in miniature.
And who wouldn't like to be a story of gadding about
as a spinning swarm about to colonize here and there
in the service of the inscrutable wisdom of hauling ass
to somewhere you can stay put come fire or high water?
It's always been about competition. Bees are bad news,
and I'm no Einstein but I'm smart enough to recognize
a threat when I see it—I show the guy where to spray.

I'd rather not be part of this or the easy metaphor it is
for exterminations taking place in the name of God

or all things good in the century of the end of oil.
I get out of the way and let a professional do his job.
I write him a check when the killing's good and done.
I make a joke: *This is why I exist, to write checks.*
I get out a broom and move the dead around some.
I sweep sand until I remember that it cleans itself.

Dixie Highway

Here date and coconut palms lean, row upon row,
propped upright by lengths of cut lumber, survivors
of last year's hurricanes, bent but straightening out
beside two-lane A1A, what locals call *Dixie Highway*.
Floridians have come to terms with sand and sand's
ceaseless gypsy blowing. But an ocean isn't a thing
you come to terms with, not ever. The dazzlement
of the waves says that, regardless of our preparation,
water gets what water wants. Date palms opening
in a flash of color isn't a thing to be bargained with,
though the air from off the Atlantic is our history—
an American history, meaning bloody. Wind's story
here is the story of slave ships; of war and huge waste.
*Way down yonder in the land of cotton, old times there are
not forgotten—look away, look away. . . .* You know the song.
Here I am making a judgment call about the guilty rule
of law that bends every day in South Florida in response
to the capricious whims and ocean sounds in the blood
and bones of the few, here where the rich enter
oblivious and leave this life ecstatic in their good fortune
while the rest drive A1A across Jupiter Island and dream.
I had parents—poor folks, and proud—I'm not crying
for food like some Sudanese orphan pestered by flies
that swarm around misfortune like the words of a story.
And I know the universe isn't fair: roads to and from
all begin, any day, in the country of backbreaking work
and low pay. I know, too, that in December the beach

at Hobe Sound will empty, pennants signaling *swim
at your own risk* snapping and flapping like mad—
the same wind that spins out the tow and undertow
washes to shore as light and litter, plastic soda bottles,
kelp-draped, arrived from God only knows how far.

Suspended Florida State Quarterback
Identifies Himself as God

TALLAHASSEE, Fla. (AP)–Suspended Florida State
quarterback Wyatt Sexton was doused by pepper spray
and taken to a hospital by police after he was found
lying in the street and identifying himself as God.

—FOXSports.com

Rule One: A residential neighborhood in Florida is no place
to be doing push-ups in the street and jumping on cars.
If you are him, the Tallahassee police want you to know

that by the time they tell you, *Get your ass on your feet, boy*
you've already crossed the line into civil disobedience.
We all know the story of that hubbub in Jerusalem,

what one *really* bad day can lead to. No one wants
that sort of thing repeated in the Sunshine State.
Rule Two: If you go to a Dave Matthews Band concert

anywhere in Tennessee, be sure to stay in Tennessee,
until the tab of Ecstasy you swallowed wears off.
Rule Three: No deity worth his weight in pepper spray

dispenses *Motherfuck you, asshole* as a form of blessing.
Rule Four: Normally, the Florida police aren't altar boys.
Rule Five: Throwing touchdowns may be miraculous,

the preferred method to achieve forgiveness of sins,
but North Florida isn't the Kingdom of Heaven—
there are rules and, by God, you'd better know them.

Leaving the Cobb Jupiter 18 Cinema Singing "Springtime for Hitler"

Sometimes all the anxieties and vanities fall away
and you trot out a lyric from a Mel Brooks' musical

for the best reason one has to sing: because it cancels
a day of rain, the Olympic-scale weight of ordinariness.

You're crossing a mall parking lot in Jupiter, Florida
as giddy as—what?—a schoolgirl? Sure, if schoolgirls

sing *Springtime for Hitler and Germany, Winter for Poland
and France. . . .* Being happy is like an eclipse reaching

the point where the cashew-crescent sliver disappears
into an unmediated ring of light. You want that first-

day-of-existence swell of feeling to keep breaking.
So you sing, *Don't be stupid, be a smarty. Come and join*

the Nazi party. But it's gone, you're you, and rain
is coming down hard, stinging. It's begun to sheet

across the windshields of cars as you rush to yours.
Inside, droplets and light river dashboard curves.

In a world that surges with as much hate as music—
more hate, come to think of it, much more—

suffering isn't that knee-slappingly funny or avoidable.
You don't weep as you turn the key, but you should.

Night Migration

Trimming knives lie in stacked *x*'s in the last yard of the day.
"Stairway to Heaven" pours from a boom box like cooler air.
Each staircase of bundled fronds is like the one Robert Plant
describes before the supervisor twists a volume knob as if he's
heard it all before—that dream of redemption / reward / afterlife
reapportioned like the idea that any of us ever buys our way
into or through a world other than this one. The light is going.
An idling Volvo truck sighs arpeggios of exhaust as workers
shake off leaf dust. One man plants himself by the boom box
to crank up the guitar solo as if some music softens hard truths.

Every evening along US 1 in South Florida, and in all seasons,
trucks carry them, engines singing of brown-skinned realities
and laboring in the groves of orange and lemon and grapefruit
or landscaping gated communities with names like Medallion,
where latter-day pirates cash in a lifetime of loot and plunder
for eleven thousand square feet of X-marks-the-spot on an acre and a half.
Those in the trucks would be the first to tell you life isn't fair,
talking to each other, themselves, as rips of sunset-pink or -red
appear in the vault of sky over Young & Prill Funeral Home.
What do I care if they're weary and climb down from a tailgate

as if a day had asked everything of them and they'd answered?
What do I know of returning to a wreck of a gold Toyota Corolla
in the dim parking lot of a Publix, having to pray for the miracle
of the internal combustion engine to again carry you to a room
with thin, pictureless walls and a wash basin? If there is a soul,

it's in men like these. Which is why some doubt—that oldest
of parlor games—the spirit's existence, given a tendency to stare
into the distance, to look off into whatever Florida coastal town
rips the bones from your back, as Bruce Springsteen sang once,
then keep looking for that heaven the first light of stars is selling.

You Must Drive This Car

How suddenly I walked from the stage of my father's life,
and because he objected to the violence in a video.
He asked me to pack and go, to leave his house—
I was 1100 miles from Ohio. Said it was about respect.
All right, I said, loading the stuff of my life.

He'd risen from the sofa, incensed, out of his mind
with those years he'd repaired Minuteman missiles.
(He carried the Cold War like a retirement watch.)
In the movie, though, the dead fell one at a time.
They weren't white or American, anything to him.

It's like this car salesman who got tired of his life
and, pressing, said, *You must drive this car!*
I told him what I told my father in Florida
as I turned to go: No one has to do shit.
I don't know. Maybe the spray of blood and brain

became present in the room—what else?—in a way
it never had when he fixed the nuclear arsenal.
But only when he rose, like the heavens had opened,
did I begin to believe he cared about anyone.
And then his soul was this shout you had to hear.

At the Wheel of the Pilar, Ernest Hemingway Addresses the Breezes off the Coast of Cuba

In his booming, amphitheatrical voice, he calls out:
Our father who art in nada, nada be thy name.

And if the wingbeats of the gulls are God's answer,
they are also the wingbeats of gulls and only that.

He keeps the .32 Smith & Wesson at his waist.
Loaded and holstered—the gun his father shot

himself with. He says the heirloom pistol
is for bull sharks. It's June, 1941. And the war

in Europe isn't being staged for this American,
but it beats offering all comers a hundred dollars to box

on the docks: bareknuckled or with the gloves.
In any war, the moon is still the moon and men

like this man up to God knows what for glory.
Everyone on the island is sleeping in the nude

and with a window open, praying for a breeze.
With a crew and a Thompson submachine gun,

again he patrols the north coast to Cayo Confites.
Again, wafers of moon transubstantiate in waves

scarving the hull in all waters, littoral and pelagic.
Again he wants to sink a U-boat with short-fuse

munitions, hand grenades. Rationed diesel fuel
feeds the 75-horse Chrysler, low engine-echo

unbuilding the dark, encouraging shore birds
to change rooms in their houses by the sea.

Live Nudes

I watch my Florida friend rake a free hand
through his buzzed-off hair, face full of sunset,
as he tells me about a tittie bar named Love Land.
Call him Jim. Jim stocks paint for Home Depot.
Went to Stetson College on a baseball scholarship.
The dashboard-glow greens a surf of horizon-pink
and Jim's face between sips from a Starbucks cup.
I love those discoveries men make about themselves
not meaning to, catcalls of self knowledge ripped
from smoke so thick it slices with a swizzle stick.
They may hear themselves become Sonny Corleone
in *The Godfather*, calling women *broads* or worse
and forgetting that respect isn't only about knowing
which new stranger's name to loose while sighing
behind dark-lensed Ray-Bans. Don't get me wrong.
I savor the idea of dioramas of long-hair-tossing
showgirls with veteran hearts, women who couldn't
care less why some men want to nuzzle a dream:
pole-proficient *b-yooties*. Still, I say, No thanks.
Jim nods, says, *It figures* and *Your loss, my friend*.
He tells me, in the glow of the dashboard LEDs,
that the women at Love Land are thrilled to death
to be doing what they're doing, naked and soaring
across the stage in a state of entrepreneurial bliss,
glimpsing a clock or plotting their children's futures.
But riding like this in his Cadillac, by a restaurant
where neon sails bloom, Jim confesses that nothing

is more fleeting than the pirate smile of a pole dancer.
Says he slipped an Andy Jackson into a G-string to see
Rapunzel ("El") vee trophy legs under a sun-and-moon
ball of mirrors. *Spinning the straw of self into gold—*
he doesn't say it like that, but that's what he means.

The Lives of My Poems after I'm Gone

Part-poems that snagged ten grand (twice) and the pages
that hauled in a Creative Writing Fellowship from the NEA
and caused twenty grand to be wired to a bank in Ohio—
those pages are out drinking beer, whoring around,
celebrating having meant something to someone once.
They're not stupid, my poems; they live in Florida.
They belly up to a tiki bar, as loud and belligerent
and self-centered as fraternity men on tabs of ecstasy.
And the love poems that brought the beloved to life—
those build bridges to other hearts, the fickle bastards.
They want to be bedded by a flight attendant who can lie,
and does, convincingly, that they're the best she's had.
They want her to leave voice mails, madly passionate
declarations that other lovers will get pissed to hear.
The political poems of heartbreak and disappointment—
they'll likely have nothing to do with the love poems,
forgetting the one country where our dreams prevail.
Maybe a few benefit from facts surrounding my death,
the timing coinciding with a cataclysm in the cosmos,
the death of a star birthing displays of some magnitude
in a dark corner of Heaven. Maybe one shakes hands
with Barack Obama on the cover of *Rolling Stone*.
The pages that won a grant from the Sunshine State—
maybe these throw a party for Peter Schmitt's poems
at some Miami nightspot, and they buy all the drinks.

Maybe they dress in gaudy Florida shirts in our honor.
Maybe one of my poems and one of Peter's get jailed
for hopping a red-eye from Miami to D.C. and taking
a long slow piss on the Capitol steps, the piss stream
shouting truth to power without benefit of words.

God's Circus at Its Wintering Grounds
in Florida

Of course it's a nondenominational outfit.
A bunch of trailers parked by Chevy Suburbans.
And I don't know the names of the animals
or one act from another, nevertheless
they'll let you walk among them if you watch
and don't trip over a colossus doing calisthenics.
Don't stare at the fire-eater's ass in spandex.

Mornings, they fall out like an army between battles.
A few build cook fires in circles that have seen their share
of junk-mail-as-kindling, Papa John's pizza coupons messaging
in flickers of combustion, white-winged butterflies flitting
through several heavens of smoke in branches overhead.

If those between jobs are beautiful, these are beautiful.
If dressing in rags is a niche sport, they're athletes.
Rescue dogs nap in pairs on heaped canvasing.
Graveyard cats come and go like light on stones.
Of course the man in charge is a woman. Tells
stories. Lets you in on the workings of a circus
before smiling and waving and volunteering you
for chores that purchase temporary membership.

Jim Morrison & The Doors in Miami, 1969

Morrison performs a series of affable pats to a cushion
on a backstage sofa. This, to signal the next woman who
loves without hope. If you sport a stiffy for all creation,
sooner or later, you take it out. Wave it at butterfingered
fandom. Before the show, a woman makes zipper noises,
emancipates him from the infamous leather pants. Which
he steps out of. Manzarek, the organist, bangs to be let in

and a joke about organ parts comes to mind. Morrison
elects to rediscover the orthodoxies of a Marlboro. First,
he thumbs a lighter wheel. Then, a hand positions flame
to the tip end of the cigarette. Zigzags of smoke become
fog-wreathed rollercoaster curves then gray boutonnieres.
This woman, his Florida guide, is from Ohio. And maybe
Miss Ohio thinks, *What's one more fall between acrobats?*

Jim Morrison isn't looking for a future with a house. Kids.
Membership in Cougar Octagon Optimist Club of Dayton.
Meaning, to him, the Buckeye State might as well be Mars.
He shakes his hair. Certain lighting adores a mane of hair.
This March night, the air is an atomization of discontent.
And so he wonders if some invisible man in the sky,
high above the strongbox that is America, fantasizes

stepping out of Paradise. Maybe needs a little time or
maybe to see if the revenant flesh ever gets to be a bore.
And not just to wheedle a welcome-back trumpet fanfare.
A eucharist of blotter LSD is bringing on the color wheel,
rainbowing the upturned face of the woman holding him.
And he smiles. Generations of dead know that smile
as reminiscent of fire shoveled by envious angels.

3

After the first death, there is no other.
—DYLAN THOMAS

Lee in the Orchard, 1865

This was after Lincoln had walked in Richmond.
It was the first week of April. There were blossoms.
Alone with the old agonies and smoldering new ones,
he may have shoved open the corset of a fence. Tied up
his horse, Traveler. And the horse may have whinnied,
the animal noise suspending midair like wood smoke.

Lee may have had to ask, *What are you doing here?*
and answer that very good question as best he could.
He knew that he had to answer Grant if not himself.
He may have walked where the promise of fruition
hung enormously still in some distant midsummer,
his apparitional army matching him step for step.

And though a hard justice had found R. E. Lee,
it was abridged by a blur of yellow jackets. Bees.
Something the heart of a flower requires like light.
Something like drops of rain if the rain had wings.
They had followed blood rivers at Chancellorsville.
Angels of the battlefield, he heard them called once

by a boy lieutenant in the Army of Northern Virginia.
If he considered what Henry (Light-Horse Harry) Lee
might have done, he told no one. And he neither smiled
nor looked in any direction where his face could be read
or decoded as having caught sight of the end of the world
as he paced under and around a buzzing of tiny live things.

"And the Blood Came Trickling Down"

The phrase doesn't occur anywhere in the Bible.
My grandmother made it up once while reading aloud.
Someone with a third-grade education and genuine faith
who liked westerns and that American gospel of flaming
clouds exploding over the heads of the meek of the earth.

Sooner or later, she'd tear up and then uncover the hem
of her petticoat to make spotless the lenses of her bifocals.

The grisly poetry of Revelations says the end of the world
is that horrific time the living envy the dead, a bad-enough
bedtime story, but that *Sturm und Drang* of the Crucifixion—
that was taking annunciatory trumpeting too far. Adlibbing
a metaphor for blood loss is one thing, but the mouths of

hellish furnaces were in that tale of violence. That gospel.
An intercessory drip drip drip—weight of self, lifting at death.

Now here in the calm autonomies of my older years
I am thinking that humankind could be less appalling.
Maybe another messiah, some variety of a pissed off Jesus,
could roll back the heavy stone of the tomb on the Fourth of July.
He (or she) could step out. Say, *Enough with the fireworks.*

A door in the heart of the world might open. A trumpet
sound. We could have a new god and new soap opera.

Black Radio

It was a Zenith Trans-Oceanic, with rows of red-orange push buttons
and serial black tuning knobs that said the path to wonder commenced
with a frequency indicator floating like a bubble in a carpenter's level.
He listened to WSM, the Grand Ole Opry—my father, Saturday nights,
drifting to sleep to Hank Snow or Roy Acuff or a bluegrass band
he could tell you the history of. Sleepwear consisted of a t-shirt
and J.C. Penney pajama bottoms. When he and my mother still
slept together, she would be awake on her side of the bed—
propped up and reading, an L&M burning in a crystal ashtray.
Telling him, *Turn it down!* until the singer's voice was a whisper.
Whatever happens when we die, suffering will have to be explained.
Maybe God will pass out the Trans-Oceanics, and the dead will huddle
around the set, listening to a cloud-nine version of a fireside chat.
Maybe she'll find him—my father—and they'll argue about volume.
I like to think we'd have hands to tune notched knobs. Eyes to judge
where the Nashville station is clear and the voices of hearts absolve us
and death is a song we automatically sing, knowing all the words.
Maybe we're dead and the trespass of living rises like so much smoke.

Jack Johnson Returns to His America to Eat Cold Eels and Think Distant Thoughts

Because the rules are what they are in America,
we love to hear about men who will not bow down,
whose gold-capped teeth reflect the paradisial and
that gambled-away glow in which we find ourselves.
But those who disparage the rule makers want power,
and one cannot love the Ur-Male without reservation
since whose fault is it that the world is a boxing ring?
Returning from exile, in newsreel footage, a reporter
asked Johnson why women (meaning, *white* women)
preferred men like him. The champion hell-raisers.
Men whose faces light hits and we see what's inside.
He said, *It's because we like to eat cold eels and*
think distant thoughts then stared, meaningfully.
Which meant that he didn't have an explanation.
When a man like that makes love, he thinks of
giving and taking beatings, of ass whippings.
O Jack, we are all knocked down and rising.
Lives are like fake-sky murals covering the
ceilings of flophouses. I read somewhere
you said your career proved that triumph
at thieving wages transforms nothing—
not bad for a boxer who collected clocks.
A man on the run from the powers that be
and time, which says what it says about each of us.
If lives speak, yours said—and I'm paraphrasing—
a man can never truly love anything over which
he has no power, especially a country so beautiful
it promises to lie and break your heart. Then does.

Truck Picture, 1962

for Suzanne

Some love is like an aperture—
hearts open and close, allow the lens
of self and memory-film to take the light
at different intensities. It's still love.

My father is smiling. There's a sign on the side
of a '57 Ford Ranchero that reads *Roy's Shell.*
An address and phone number in red-lettered script.
He's at the wheel, window down. My sister Suzanne
calls attention to a shadow, a vertical-running line.
As from tape. As if the negative was ripped. Torn.

And I remember blood flowing from his face after
she struck him—that time, for bringing a woman
along. They were divorcing but would remarry.
That night, he was stopping by to drop me off.
That weekend, my sisters hadn't gone with him.
I recall that he opened my door. Said, *Hurry!*

I'm sure the woman was sitting next to him.
I'm sure she was difficult to get to because
my mother tried to reach across me to hit her
and hit me. I come from those who strike first,
which is to say, my mother did. Her mother,
my granny, absorbed a blow. Cried and cried.

The violence of desire is understandable but tough
to do much about if you're a kid. I see my father

tearing out of the driveway, sparks arcing up
from underneath the Ranchero, rooster-tailing
into an Ohio night I enter again and again,
trying to snap and frame a picture I trust.

Byron and Shelley, Maintaining

It's Mary Shelley's idea that they swallow hallucinogens,
the gift of some vicar-general friend, an herbal Ecstasy
this daughter of Mary Wollstonecraft ingests as well.

These are deists. Like Jefferson, seeing God in all things.
To say that the drug then allows them to open themselves
to an experience of deity would be redundant, and a lie.

In an hour, Byron is talking Greek revolution to a plant,
the plant seeming to evidence great political understanding.
Shelley attempts to inscribe *P.B. Shelley* on a sheet of water

in a serving tray. On her back, looking up at a black ceiling,
Mary glimpses a Promethean monster with the pilfered heart
of a hanged man. A golem with huge shoes. She's laughing;

that is, they take turns erupting at some new truth about being.
It could be argued that Percy Bysshe Shelley is making a noise
like rattling coins, a sound in praise of the entire transaction.

For some reason, Byron decides that he and Shelley should
be serious. He says they are, after all, famous English poets.
Says it as if John Keats himself had walked into the room

reciting from "Bright Star": *Awake for ever in a sweet unrest,*
Still, still to hear her tender-taken breath, / And so live ever—
or else swoon to death. . . . Deathclothes walking and a voice.

Shelley appears chastened. Rights himself by the fireplace.
Byron asks for a mirror to comb his hair, which is mussed.
And so, with a flourish, Shelley empties the serving dish,

hands the heirloom silver tray to his friend. Who takes it;
says, mockingly, *A poet must always appear at his best.*
To which Mary responds by spewing a mouthful of wine.

Beautiful Ohio

When the guy who fixes the stopped-up toilet
and stalled gas furnace says he's from Lithopolis
but uses the word *hillbilly* in a derogatory way,
I'm not certain why I chose the Buckeye State
to start over again. He does try to backpedal
when I tell him that I'm one, and proud of it.
He says he likes moonshine. Makes his own.
I tell him that my folks were from Kentucky.
I let place names roll off my tongue like praise
for Jesus or Elvis. The little shit wears Oakleys
tilted back on a crew-cut head. He's confident
of a share of a place in the world. And smiles.
I get close to him when we talk. Real close.
I want him to know I'm likely to do anything.
When he asks why anyone with college admits
to being from Appalachia, I know I'm home—
where my parents felt the winds of loneliness
like the breath of the departed but never left.
And I do what they would've done: I shake
the man's hand. I open the door for him.

White Cane Lying in the Gutter in the Lane

—NEIL YOUNG, "Don't Let It Bring You Down,"
After the Gold Rush

Okay, so it's 1970. October. The new Neil Young album
has come out. I'm holding my copy, the night-black record
minus the sleeve and jacket—holding it like I've been taught
by my audiophile father. One of those use-the-coaster guys.
A bastard. Not in the sense of being a cruel man, not yet,
but raised without a father. Poor. And in the Army at sixteen.
He's someone who doesn't waste much. And he's said,
Hold a record by its edges and I didn't—after—and
got bawled out. So it's something I do. Even stoned.
Sixteen years old, I'm tripping. Carrying *After the
Gold Rush* by its edges to a turntable. I will need,
soon, an unswerving voice to track for a few hours.

By the seventh cut of the album, my white bedspread—
an advertisement white-white J.C. Penney chenille one—
is transmuting. First, into a python. Then, a man's cane.
Now the cane writhes in and through the transparent air
of Ohio, this after the shooting at Kent State that May.
I see the cosmos in that snake-cane. Feel electricity.
A tremor that, then, trips up the spine. And outward.
I hear Neil Young saying I am not to let it, the mess
of the world, bring me down. As if anyone has his
or her shit together like that: enough to just smile
and let time be compressed into a spiritual spiral
galaxy that spins in and through blind America.

A Palestinian Boy Looks through the Rubble inside His Home in a Refugee Camp near Tyre

. . . thinking quietly how surely heaven must have something of the color and shape of whatever village or hill or cottage of which the believer says, This is my own.

—WILLIAM FAULKNER, *Light in August*

There's a kid wearing an orange t-shirt
in a room of gauzy, scavenger sunbeams.
And a burst wall with its window intact.
And a Lebanese flag with a green cedar
brazing the air above block after block
of bombed-out houses. Maybe he hears
shrieking from catacombs in the collapse,
maybe audible voices and a dog barking.
If Heaven is an echo of our last home here,
a window opening onto a hillside orchard
where trees sag from their summer weight,
then a contingent of new arrivals is blissful,
believing there can be no sinful act on earth
for which they will not be forgiven. Maybe
the boy is recalling a man and white poodle
walking the streets, unhurried in predawn,
another partisan who'd been screwing and
taking God's name in vain until a whirring
like unhived, angry bees halted all interest
and he headed, far too late, for the shelter.
If he comes back to the wreck of childhood

with a notion of putting things in perspective,
what seems large to a boy won't be to the man.
Seeing differently changes objects, landscapes.
Memory's precincts invariably transubstantiate
into a crummy hill at the edge of a ruined city.
Nonetheless, he may want a token from that hill.
Maybe he finds a rock which his man's closed-
hand just about covers, and the stone carries
the hard smell of skin after he holds it. Skin
and the pleasures of being anyone humming
his national anthem. If the hill is a temple,
then the token is its miniature. A reminder
of limits, an end of one thing and a beginning.
Presence. Geological time. He may appreciate
the way one can seemingly cancel the other
before they become inseparable and the same.
And for as long as light moves this afternoon,
the glow on his ziggurat of rubble is a clock.

The Nascent Soul Selects a Set
of Appalachian Parents

There's this ledge you look over. A railing you lean out from
and stare down at a world of souls like the feeder at Sea World.
And I didn't know a hillbilly from dark matter, a skewered star,
looking down beside a hallelujah gallery of bureaucrat angels.
My soon-to-be parents would move from Kentucky to Ohio,
so I wouldn't go hungry as a kid. And I wouldn't have to be
referred to, unfavorably, in comparisons to a coal bucket.
So what if I didn't know my ass from a glass of buttermilk.
So what if I'd lug a Southern accent around like a school bag.

A box of rocks might have had more walking-around sense,
but I was sure that I'd be happy—the way he looked at her
and the way she looked back at him like we'd be all right.
A family. And if it didn't happen this way, it could have.
Who can say that it didn't? I mean, there's all this talk
of a heaven they've gone to now, having left the body.
I'm just saying it works both ways. Or that it should.
I'm saying any given heaven goes by several names.
And one of those is a synonym for Fleming-Neon.

Einstein and Chaplin at the Movies

In black tie, the two are attending a premiere of *City Lights*.
The collapse of the German currency is being reported,
so Hitler and the Third Reich are in the wings, so to speak.

Relativity is responsible for the presence of one man,
all the properties of light for the other. At the podium
before microphones each jokes—Chaplin whispers

a question about the eclipse of 1919, the tendency of light
to curve as it passes through a strong gravitational field.
Einstein grins as they shake hands for the newsreels.

For years, Albert Einstein has been trailing headlines—
Revolution in Science. Newtonian Ideas Overthrown—
and extramarital affairs to rival even Charlie Chaplin.

It doesn't take a biographer to tell you that Einstein
may be recalling the last starlet to murmur *Albert*
as he inhaled the hypotenuse of her blond triangle.

The trick to success in America is knowing which
movie mogul will protect you when the time comes,
who to slip a folded Franklin *not* to print your picture.

Long after doors at the back of the theater are opened,
the overflow famous disappeared by exits, ushers report
this winter afternoon in nineteen thirty-one trailed off

with marquee light bright on the gem-studded leash
of a poodle dragged to obedience by a chauffeur
whose huge patience was tried once too often.

WD8RBB

You were a ham radio operator, WD8RBB your call sign.
When you died, neighbors took apart the antennae tower
like stories about someone having outlandish, circus sex
with a willing stranger. The tower sold for a good price.

Deep into grief for my mother, once I heard you praying
as if someone was listening in a paradise whose call sign
only the unborn and the true believer commit to memory.
After, you might start coughing or go into the bathroom.
Minus distortion or atmospheric interference, a message
of dire warning seemed to flash from a rubble of throat.

We had eavesdropped, you and I, on the Thrilla in Manila
on a Trans-Oceanic Zenith beside your amateur radio gear.
That drama traveled to us by the refraction of radio waves.
Existence and oblivion are pugilists, Ali-Fraziers contesting
the likelihood we're here and gone. Remember that family
who lived down the street when I was a kid, the Kostas?

They acted, rain or shine, as if being alive is the problem.
I recall them acknowledging—with all their mad pointing
and yelling in ballpark-angry American English and their
native Greek—that talk is not just talk or silence silence.

American Christian

This was the first time I had seen her kneel like that.
Both her black shoes were off. And I recall her nylons
drooped in the soles of her feet as she raised her hands
like the sparsely furnitured bedroom was a planetarium
and humbling herself the way to crank open a row house
roof to Kentucky night sky so full of stars it glistened.

She was petitioning Heaven, showing me how to pray.
And got cranked up. Rattled off her name and mine,
the address in Neon, like God needed coordinates
to locate the two of us in the deep end of the pool
of believers. Kneeling like that in the lamplight,
my grandmother Mazy Frances Collier Potter

might have been Lillian Gish, silent movie star.
I had bought a paperback biography of Lillian Gish.
After I read it to her, parts of it, she said sound ruined
the movies. That it would have been better, the world—
translation: Neon, Kentucky—without it. Eventually,
she broke off praying. Raised herself from the floor.

And reached for a black Bible so her finger might
locate and trace the red-lettered verses on the pages.
Then she read aloud—haltingly—like someone
prized for the hard use to which she had put her body:
a woman with a third-grade education ready to answer
direct questions but never to volunteer an opinion.

The Pop-up Book of Falling in Love

Here is the stiff-paper equivalent of the look passed.
And here is wanting every asked-for thing answered.
She sees him in the morning mirror of her looking.
And he sees her. Both freeze-frame the restlessness
that attends an emptiness about to fill with desire.
What is happening happens as the background tabs
on the cardboard cutouts do an earthquake dance
then disconnect. This is how happiness begins—
with *Yes, oh yes.* Isn't that autumn in the Midwest
there in the pasteboard foreground? Aren't those
oak and maple leaves at the feet of the lovers?
But isn't a rainbow on the leaf-faces a bit much?
A promise-come-unstuck moment seeds futures
by subtracting the world from around raised faces.
First the moment, and then the need. It helps
if each is honeycombed with need. Then at least
one key has to turn in the deadbolt of the door
to a dark, four-chambered cardstock heart—
you there, turn the page. Let these fold closed
and let other forms resurrect, signaling the truth
that their book of lives was unbodied till now.

James Dean Kissing Julie Harris
in *East of Eden*

Now the better future has its say.
Now the lovers open their mouths

of once-only flesh saying: *Take this*
longing in fair exchange for yours.

Cal, eager to earn his way, shamed
for having an old whore for a mother

then not so much disgraced as reborn
into a world where fortunes rise and

fall with the market value of beans.
The message: God would have to be

a dumbass of some cosmic magnitude
to favor dweeb-son Aron over this guy,

Cal, maybe not the good son but a hunk
of scorching lust to succeed, nonetheless.

That the object of Cal's affection is his
brother Aron's girl is her call, after all.

Free will means everything is up for grabs.
And maybe he's dumbstruck by the offer.

But the kiss is in case there's no heaven,
no God, this appalling existence a single

CinemaScope *Paradise Lost* upon which
to bestow any sort of hope of redemption.

What's a boy to do but smooch the girl
and outshine Adam for good measure.

America as Ex

About the 1776th time I begged her not to spend money
we didn't have and she ignored me—we're not together.
But if we talk on the phone, I'll start in wanting her back.
Lately, however, I'm hearing the language of despotism.
A dismissal of the sorrow of others. For as long as I've
known her, her vibrator War—that's what she calls it—
has been her dearest tool. Before, her Federal Reserve
Bank of infidelities might have been almost defensible,
but then she whined, *The effing poor are such a pain.*

To say you loved her, in those days, was to place
yourself in contention. Because you wanted what
she wanted, which was everything. I loved her then.
But I'm prepared to watch her walk over the skyline,
waving off the exceptional distance ahead and behind.
I see buds she brings to flowering, that history. And can
identify some in Ohio in spring, though I hate accounting
for that weed-heart. Whatever else, screamers like her
are all about pain. And some love will get you killed.

Herons, in April in Ohio

These wade development lakes, stirring
malnourished reeds like revelatory winds.

Thieving sustenance, they move like a hand
on an abacus, the *click-click-click* of mouths
keeping track in the calculus of the shallows.

Noise levels equivalent to carousels in endless
revolution, these build the unbuilt world. Nests
are the usual archive of ground litter. Ephemera.
Kroger grocery sacks are gorgeous with new use.

Not even the beautiful can answer for the poison—
the hanging veil of semitruck exhaust by the road,
apparitional fracking rigs taller than the church spire,
environmental refutations of the barely probable soul.

Once more, the birds have had to become American
in their capacity to coexist with the lack of respect
for everything. In the golds of sunset, I go down
and walk and wish for the healing to come soon.

If this were your last hour, wouldn't you want
the herons to stand upright in light like this?

Wouldn't you want to sigh them out into air
and watch them glide to an alternate world
above our immoderate worship of makers
and jackhammers that stagger the birds?

Death at the Lakeshore

Truth be told, I took the job for the perks—
deathlessness, mostly—and wound up afoot
in the heart of the day in my black ankle-top
Converse All Stars, shepherding the good
and the fucked to places I couldn't believe
where gargoyles sing "Imagine" a capella.

Bookkeeping and scheduling are daunting,
but I can't hold their tardiness against them.

On the lakeshore, wind has a close voice
that reshapes dissatisfactions. This morning
it shuffled pages of the *Cleveland Plain Dealer*—
the sports section feature on Browns football.
The geese waddle-walked on the newspaper
in a light that says what happens is random

and a few loops and knots of enduring time
you enter to leave forever. I come for them.

There really is no such thing as dying well.
I may hear inanities like *I smell chocolate*
or *I need to drive to a grocery tomorrow*
or *I'm not the only one naked in the room*
and then they simply stop breathing. Those
alive in autumn by a lake will want to exit

in September, the sugar maples reddening
as a group before mislaying their leaves.

Go quickly, travel safely, my young friend, to the land of ghosts.

—Knock in *Nosferatu*, 1922

Puberty

I'm twelve. In my pj's at Gary Laberman's house on Comanche Drive.
We're loud-chomping popcorn from a Tupperware bowl, when the son
of Frankenstein calls that gorgeous Promethean apostasy, the Monster,
my father's work, talking theatrically in a detached tone of voice.

The Good Doctor sounds like he's going through puberty. Gary and I
are sprouting hair on our gonads, having started the sex ed classes
with our dads, watching arabesques of microscopic sperm jigging up
fallopian tubes on rapturous journeys toward making life. The son

of the maker of monsters, new deed holder to Castle Frankenstein,
names the lightning-play in the picture window. Calls it magnificent.
There are torches. Igor lights one in a crypt where a living-cadaver
colossus sleeps on the slab above Baron von Frankenstein's grave.

And, later, there are sparking machines with chain-draped histories.
The lighting in *Son of Frankenstein* is like the black-and-white films
we watch in the sex education classes. Gary's seen them, too. He's
been there, in an auditorium/gym, with a dad staring straight ahead

so he won't have to make eye contact with anyone. It's shyness,
sure, and magnificent, but we're not there right now. Not hearing
how the man puts his penis in the woman's vagina, not hearing
what good it is, knowing what to do with a body you don't own yet.

Gary has his hand in the Tupperware. He's transfixed as Igor starts
lecturing the son as to what it takes to carve your name into the face

of Heaven and the eternal. Of course there's no rest for anyone whose
superhuman heart thrums along at two hundred fifty beats per minute,

the speed of the heart of a boy upon first hearing the word *intercourse*.
In a year or two, we know we'll be the monster who stalks little girls.
Any day, our phalluses will accept the cosmic jolt of time, and grow.
Any minute, we're certain, townsfolk will start lighting the torches.

Astonished Man

Richard Matheson: The author and screenwriter is the man Collier runs into as he is leaving the bathroom after shaving and looks astonished at him, hence his billing as an Astonished Man.

—IMDb, the trivia to *Somewhere in Time*

Chance Locke's wife Rose says a sphere of light,
a blue light *with zigzags*, arrived in the room,
his dog, the one he'd named after Dorothy's—
a talcum-white toy poodle version of *her* Toto—
that dog barking at the light or the presence
of death, or both, though death is always
present under white fluorescent-lit walls
and doesn't seem to mind being the center
of attention. Everyone in Florida at least
dies warm, so he had *that* going for him.
And a doting wife who hovered, twisting
the ephemeral and mysterious into a shape
recognizable at once. Even his first name
was a grammar of expectation of unheralded
good, the honed moment of unbearable happiness
that waltzes in from nowhere or Pennsylvania,
cocking a Panama hat and motioning for a chair
to be moved closer. You know what I mean—
Chance is all about what's not out of the question.
No saint, this one had a reverence for the light:
the ways it falls onto downturned orchid petals—
he raised white Dendrobium orchids in slatted
wood boxes hung from the sides of date palms.

The zigzags may have been a hesitating, having
a look at his boxed flowers or the wind-denuded
bougainvillea yet climbing one wall of his house.
Then again, it may have been a ball of nothing.
But according to Rose Locke, some of us pass
from this life as if a vessel of sorts is emptying
of a grand mystery, the blue and zigzagging fact
of that display forcing eyes to open, at least one
truth given a context it lacked until that instant.

God Shows Up in Iowa

for Karla Braig

God: a being or object believed to have more than natural attributes and powers and to require human worship; specifically: one controlling a particular aspect or part of reality. . . .

—Merriam-Webster online

I know what you're thinking: This is some crackpot headline
from a Hawkeye TV news channel to get attention or ratings or both.
But he showed up, I swear. Had his left arm caught to the elbow
under the hood of a Cadillac, an older model he said he was buying.
This was in the driveway next door to my house. It was cold. Freezing.
I had gone out by a different door. Had seen him there. Just standing.

I'd opened the door. Heard him say, *Maybe you'd help me out here.*
He had been struggling but now stopped twisting his twig of a forearm.
Explained: because his arm was so thin, the thick hood had been able
to close, or nearly, and he'd been pinned but the arm hadn't broken.
He was calm. Later, he told me he'd simply *decided* to stay that way.
This was an Abe Lincoln of a guy in khakis, a sweatshirt and sweater.

No coat. Arms bare. Like he hadn't intended to wind up found out—
outside, which in winter in Iowa means you need more than one coat—
and found out to be the Almighty. Why God? A couple of reasons.
First: no crowd gathered. (It was him and me.) A kid he had gotten the

attention of—an hour earlier, when it first happened—had wandered off. Second: he hummed to himself while I jiggled the huge Cadillac hood.

When it popped opened—the big hood—there wasn't a spot on the arm. By definition, that in itself should be enough. Right? There's a word— that word is *godding*—for elevating the everyday to the status of divine. And maybe that's what I'm doing. But then I was doing something else, something other than falling short of the fact that we lack good sense. That day, I went out the wrong door at the right time, and saved a life.

When Billie Holiday Sings
about Southern Trees

and blood on the leaves, you see the congruent drip
inscribe moonlit ground. You smell old magnolias.
The piano plays a dirge; the trumpet plays one, too.
The weight of wrong is in the voice that soars and
explodes an idea that our burdens are inert things
too heavy to lift. Everything about blood flowers.
And the knots and cordage a lynched man strains
against before the longing in every muscle relaxes.
She's singing, *Here is a fruit for the crows to pluck*
and we hear the creak of a branch accepting a rope.
We hear the awful noise that is like no hinge singing.
After we imagine this, what goes out from each of us
isn't like breath. It's more a needing to look away
before making a eucharist of regret. Take this song.
The essential miracle isn't that old movie of pain
with the torch singer sporting an orchid in her hair,
the dead heroine with her history of tragic stardom.
It isn't an angelic-voiced immortal or the song itself.
The miracle is we use it to redeem part of the world.

The Fury of a Patient Man

He hadn't a clue about how to be an uncle
but spoke to me in that soft-as-a-cat's-fur voice
over breakfast the year he lived with us. It wasn't
so much that the world rested on his shoulders
as that he had a conscience about what happens
to a boy becoming a man. It had happened
to him. He wanted me to hear how it'd been
growing up a boy whose first steps each day
fell, in winter, on icy linoleum in a row house
and I wanted to know. Born in a coal town,
I don't think he knew his father beyond a slap
across the face or a string of harsh words.
I'm pretty sure he wanted to warn me because
no one had said, *Don't quit school, Billy* or
tried to explain the ellipsis of human nature
as including fuckers and fuckees, which he said
was one of the lessons at the School of Hard
Knocks Upside the Head. The truth, however,
went deeper than row houses or poverty or greed
or his own contempt for talkativeness and words.
His white Impala had blunted fins, Ohio plates,
a bite-wing imprint in the metal of the fender
that matched the mouth of a would-be thief
who managed to get as far as the bar parking lot
with the keys and my uncle's wallet. Bill Potter,
my good-hearted blood relative, overtook him
and settled the score before calling my father

from a pay phone in the bar, saying, *Bring me
my pistol*. What I know of this I recall because
I saw my uncle asleep next morning on the bunk
below mine, his bruised face flashing the wide smile
of a man who, after a beating, can stand and walk.

With the Lights of Houses
Flashing By in the Darkness

The dash light threw greenish shadows across his face,
and when I looked over at him I'm sure I saw him flinch.
He let off the gas. Depressed the clutch. Shifted gears.
Squeezed the shifter knob tighter than he needed to,
the red ball of the knob, as if pissed about something.
Outside, a night of blue-black tree branches unrolled
and he reminded me of my mother's brother Billy

who took me fishing as if it was the thing to do
drag a kid along who questioned the blue of the sky.
In 1961 it felt good to be a boy in the company of men.
My father seemed pleased I was there. Glad I was glad
to be beside him for an hour. And I tried to hide away
in some lopsided instant of approval and fatherly love
as another white silo bloomed in my peripheral vision.

But when his eyes softened that night into something
resembling affection, it was as if that much emotion
was about to carry us. As if we were nearly nothing,
and a sort of general lightness of being was lifting
a man and boy on a road swelling with distances.
A kid asking if Ohio is Ohio at night and a dad
nodding and smiling, saying he didn't know.

Dressing after Sex

A pair of Holsteins wander by an electric fence
toward a promised-land red barn, the ambient noises
and their quiet beast-calm unbound in a wash of light.
And an imprint of percussive traffic sounds nearby.

This and the flood of what drags two people down
by a buckeye named American horse-chestnut.
The woman sees her hand on a pair of Levi's
and thinks, *This has cost me the life I had.*

To her right, an index finger strafes an ankle.
He'd been almost as attentive as she hoped.
Maybe this is how the habit of love begins.
Maybe it starts with handing over a shoe.

She would smile if she weren't righting herself
and reaching forward to the blanket's border
for what she never took as part of gladness:
the dispensation of joy in September grasses.

The Days of Miracle and Wonder

These are the days of miracle and wonder
This is the long-distance call. . . .

— PAUL SIMON, "Graceland"

Then this sunbeam broke through the peephole
in the front door and traveled down a long hallway
to plaster a circle on a wall at the far end of the house.
A ring about the size of a man's fist or a Florida orange.
I know nothing about the physics of light through a prism
and I don't understand the first thing about enlightenment,
but I knew enough to stand for some time before moving on.
I didn't genuflect, though this happened in Catholic Dubuque,
where I lived hoping someone would show up and save me.
Then the ray of sun-through-a-peephole disappeared and
what constitutes glowing in the Midwest in late November
along the Upper Mississippi River valley in eastern Iowa
vanished. Like those first startling moments after waking.
Like the poems the dead write using a part of morning.

Nosferatu Exits the Garden State Parkway
to Gas Up at the Wawa in Barnegat

I'm as likely to feed in Jersey as in Brooklyn.
I pull to the pump. Brake. Kill the engine.
I roll down a window of the Testarossa.
A uniform that reads *Wawa* and *Ed*
in name-eggs asks and so I say: *What?*—
Testarossa? It means 'red head' in Italian.
At a BP in Iowa, some Hawkeye drooled
on the hood. All light walkers are like that:
unworthy of antecessors who'd have bought
and driven memorable cars had they inhabited
enough darknesses to know to invest
early in Apple. Waiting, I think: the boats
of red cells, navies of them. And white-cell
sharks and platelet cuttlefish easing through
reefs of claret-colored plasma. All negotiations
regarding death involve observable movement,
so I hand over a Citibank VISA and say, *Fill it.*
The attendant says to reach down on the floor
and pull the gas-tank-cover release. And I do.
A cruiser pulls in. Flips on lights. By the *free*
air sign, serial brightnesses assault the senses.
The cop is knocking to say that I've turned right
on red. She gifts me with the oh-so-familiar nod,
flashing an oversized Atlantic states best smile
to say, *It's good you've got New Jersey plates.*
I see a platelet phalanx on the move, begetting

a general ruthlessness causing everything else.
The uniformed attendant mouths, *Check-this*,
elbow jabbing the pump worker, who stares
in a battering of wings of snow and wind
in which I hear Dante Alighieri saying,
No one thinks of how much blood costs.

O, Kindergarten

This is the classroom, a land of Crayolas
and nap time where platoons of inside voices
identify which bodily function requires answering
by raising the appropriate number of fingers
into the air of 1960. Take this quiet child.
Take a good look at something in his face.
He's been coloring the same standard-sized
sheet of milk-white paper for fifteen minutes,
and he lacks one cotton-ball blossom of a corner
before he can call it a day. But is black a color?
The truth is that it's in the carton of the box of eight,
where undersides are flattened to prevent rolling.
To him, the statuary stick figures are Eskimos
bundled to the point of facelessness in parkas of
moonless night. Which is the explanation he hopes
rescues him from the teacher with the dark down
above her upper lip, a woman bending to offer
the bald fact that black is all colors absorbed
and so it's not a color. Not in the usual sense.
A pigment. Her wide open eyes are a future
of shift after shift of feeding unpolished metals
into a polisher with the threat of layoff or firing
a black possibility. Her bland pronouncement
is the foreman telling him to get the lead out,
ordering him to work the overtime he's offered.
And not to give him any lip, no sir. What's rare
and irresistible about the kid isn't overlooked;

it's like the shadow made by a fence, any fence—
something extra. It isn't required, but he blushes
as he brushes back a lock of hair and hands her
what he calls "Eskimo, Walking at Midnight."
She holds it like it's the body of something feral.
Dead. His father's paid good money for the look
Miss White gives him that might as well be a slap.
At six, he's already been back-handed once or twice.
There's a look of his own he's crafted as answer.

Mexican Clowns Deny Costumed Killer of Drug Trafficking Boss Belonged to Their Profession

—The Washington Post

About what you'd expect a clown to say, given
that they panic tots and toddlers as often as amuse.
You can't expect a confession that the getaway car
was crowded to bursting with accomplices, a scent
of high explosives masked by a reek of grease paint.

So what if a billowy garment begs to be a chance
for inventive concealment. It doesn't mean a holster
for a SIG Sauer with silencer is sewn into every lining,
or a nylon adjustable two-point sling with the HK hooks.
Suppose the lie is part cover story to protect methods

and practices, an Agency assassin's first line of defense.
Doesn't it make sense not to throw out the crying baby
with the tepid bathwater that has served its purpose?
Ask anyone pandering for laughs for a living whether
they harbor the fantasy of biting the hand that feeds.

Let's entertain—forgive a circus pun—the idea
that access to a target had to hinge on misdirection
and surprise as much as lethality and proximity.
How often can a rosy, bulbous nose invite scorn
without wanting, at least once, to even the score?

The Mountain Elvises Get Ready
for Talent Night

A white Imperial they pull up in has four doors.
Fins as sharp as a shark's tooth. They're halved,
hillbilly-huge, bending to leave the crowded car.

The importance of being Elvis cannot be separated
from charities of light sprung from sequined capes,
fluency in Presley, a language premised on *uh-huh*
as the shibboleth for entry into the house of love.

Not one of the impersonators sees Kentucky rain,
actual rainfall in the Bluegrass State, as metaphor.
What delivery man with a respectable tenor voice
and a snarl answers a belief in sex as reparation?

In a glow of beer signs, counterfeit Ann-Margrets
wait tables. One cries as she purrs "In the Ghetto"
and gossips, *Those are real pork chop sideburns.*

G

Once, my father told me George Washington had been a Mason
and had been the Worshipful Master of his lodge while president.
He brought out a bible, my pops, flipped to George in an apron.
Said the apron was sheepskin. And that they buried him in it.
He said if I wanted to become a Mason all I had to do was ask.
I paraphrased Woody Allen quoting Groucho about not wanting
to belong to any group that would actually have me as a member.
He asked if I thought Groucho Marx was a communist. Said
that communists couldn't be Masons because they're atheists.
I heard a longing to be mollycoddled by a governable Universe.
To be affirmed as right and a believer. It was summer, Ohio,
and Marvin Gaye was on the TV in the living room, singing.
It was clear he wanted me to know what the G on his ring
stood for. He couldn't just tell me without violating an oath.
I'd turned twenty-six. Had become a father myself. I could deduce
the generational buzzing in his brain as having everything
to do with his being born out of wedlock—fatherless—
and having a son and grandson. There was something so
American in his self-glorying and in the shy way he spoke,
what would any son do but nod and turn up Marvin Gaye?

And the World All Leaves and Morning Air

—JACK GILBERT, "Bring in the Gods"
(from *Refusing Heaven*)

Though the best hour isn't one that accelerates, it might be.
And if there is anything like pleasure in recalling that day
it begins with her touching my face as she let me lift her,
the naked human skin become birdsong. Branch noises.

She'd decided on a shaded place by a bike path. Pointed.
The Lord gives everything and charges by taking it back.
What a bargain. I'm sure I thought this would be like that.
She was married. Said that her body was not hers to give

without substantial guilt. Threat of excuses, explanations.
Which she mastered by looking down and away, the asterism
of her short hair the color of camellias. Light wreathed us.
Shadows from the leafing canopy overhead wore a halo

as if the runes we leave aren't about love or language
but decipherable as longing played out in late June.

The Color Yellow, Love,
the Fall of Leaves in Autumn

*Jorge Luis Borges believed that "poetry is something
that cannot be defined without oversimplifying it. It
would be like attempting to define the color yellow,
love, the fall of leaves in autumn."*

—EDWARD HIRSCH, "From A Poet's
Glossary: Poetry" (poets.org)

Some days in May, a sunrise of redbuds will apron the clouds
and light pour across development lawns gold with dandelions.
My father told me living with others was a matter of knowing
when to weed and when to mow. I don't know how he woke
without fail at 6:10, Monday through Friday, year after year.
How he got ready for work—showered, shaved—and collected
a prepared-ahead-of-time sack lunch and a Thermos of coffee.
Sleeping in was a poor excuse for working to retire in Florida
where the shirts-on-the-clothesline May air just isn't the same.
Mother said the light there was numbing, in the Sunshine State,
but she respected my pops whose idea it'd been to move there.
Love was working like he did. Love was keeping his clothes
laundered. Setting that brown-bag lunch where he expected it.
In the Florida town where they lived he said he missed autumn.
The settling-to-earth of leaves. Seeing oaks and maples scrawl
reds and yellows like signatures across the fall sky above lawns,
by the stop sign on Lucky Avenue and State Route 79. He hated
poetry. Called it useless, though his world stank of moments
that overfill houses like the scent of coffee brewing the hour
before light clothes you and you set off to weed and mow.

One Wench in the House between Them

They lived together on the Bank side, not far
from the playhouse, both bachelors;
lay together; had one wench in the house
between them which they did so admire.

—JOHN AUBREY

for Kevin and Martha Michael

On meeting, Neal Cassady asks Jack Kerouac
about a rhythm that begins in the wires
above a road at dawn, wind just right,
and whether it has anything to do with bop
or the whereabouts of God. Jack, smiling,
says that Allen Ginsberg, jacking off
in an East Harlem apartment, heard
a voice he attributed to William Blake.
Neal, Holy Goof, can throw a football
sixty yards in a nautilus-like tight spiral,
run the hundred in under ten, jump twenty-three feet
dead still. Says he can please three women
in synchronous rotation for days and days.
When I finished my first book, Jack one-ups,
I fingered this thin hole in the ground,
fucked Ozone Park. Neal: *I can see that.*

———————

In the loft on Russell Street in San Francisco,
Jack types, stops. Cable car noises in the streets
punctuate a simple-covenant purer jazz of night—

idleness. Neal and Carolyn Cassady couple below.
Carolyn's sweet come cry anthem, within hearing,
insists, though Eisenhower is president,
that this be shared. *Come down, Jack,* they say.
This land is not the sweet home that it looks.
They burn who are living. Come down.

———————

After *On the Road,* three locals follow Kerouac
from the Kettle of Fish Bar in the Village;
they stop traffic to take turns at the famous face.
Staggering to hospital, Jack watches East Thirteenth Street,
a gray tide and light, become a junked-out
Mexican woman, Esperanza Villanueva,
who sold morphine. A dark, bilingual angel.
Your name means Hope, he'd meant to tell her.

———————

Black night seas are the centers of the eyes
of a Portuguese woman Kerouac promises
one hundred dollars the year before he dies
to gaze, for an hour, back at him. The hour
the two sit, half-candle in a saucer the only light,
the woman's lover sleeps heavily beside her
on a throw of pillows, defeating the concentration
and connection. It's the intimacy he wants:
someone, anyone, to halt the thieving future
and return everything. After, he hears
I have done this thing and pays her.

Far

Tonight, I'm reading to my grandmother Potter who
only attended school as far as the third grade. I read her
the opening pyrotechnics of the book of Revelation,
and I know Granny really wants me to read myself
to sleep, but I'm not that sleepy. I read on. There's some
Old Testament story of King David that I've flipped to
that mentions foreskins and Philistines. Farther on, these
same Philistines are having to hand over their foreskins,
so of course I ask what all that means. She tells me that
I'm circumcised, which just means *cut down there.*
She lowers her bifocals. And points and says the word
tallywacker and we laugh. She likes for me to read aloud
but doesn't like me to ask her what words mean because
it causes her to have to say, *That's far enough for tonight*
and then revisit the sad fact she doesn't know that much
about language beyond how far to take it, which is pretty
far, since she is building a life on the words. She won't
cut her hair or drink liquor or say *those* words, words
you know without me saying, because she is far enough
along in her revelation to think she shouldn't. Which is
sort of odd to my mind. I like beer and she tells the story
of having to church-key open a can of Budweiser for me.
At two, I had my very own can of beer. Anyway, I put my
heart and soul into reading. I travel to far-off Jerusalem.
I hear about the Crucifixion and the resurrection. I think
The Gospel According to Mazy Frances Collier Potter,
but what I know is that my parents are divorced and
in 1962 not one of the families on our street will let

their kids play with me. I'm pretty sure the ones
Jesus came to save aren't worth saving. Far from it.
Any kid who reads aloud from the King James Bible
thinks he's as smart as Bugs Bunny or the Road Runner.
Thinks he knows something only he knows. For example:
adults are a danger to themselves and others, and prone
to turning all creation upside down like a piggybank.
Then she tells me you can't make someone love you.
Which is damn smart for anyone who didn't make it
far beyond the third grade and who keeps her false teeth
in a glass by her bedside and keeps knocking the glass
over but can't finally figure how far is too far to reach.

My Father's Love Letters

It was 1959. Whatever had possessed my mother
to drag out the charcoal grill and pour starter fluid
over a rubber-banded stack of white envelopes,
her actions assumed the tempo of panic. Fingers
of flame shot up toward the match in her hand,
blue-yellow and swelling, spreading outward
like the hands of a pianist, the blackening scraps
rising into Ohio afternoon. Oh, and she was crying
as the smoke suggested that in a clock's tick a life
can ignite and go up. I remember she walked

from the burning pile, left me to take over.
Anything can be justified by a child's need
to know what is happening, although the lump
of smoldering intimacies inventoried feelings
I was years from having. As charred as they were,
the center mass of the letters was salvageable.
I two-fingered out a handful of envelopes.
Waved away the smoke. Grief is tissue-like—
an envelope stamped *Par Avion* testifying
to great distances. I read a few. The house

on Comanche Drive held three people then.
One of them—my father—brought currency
from Okinawa: hundred-yen notes with faces
advertising faraway fatherlands like billboards.
Adoration burns. And it keeps burning if you

go inside to your room and retrieve things
to feed the flames. All afternoon, I fed it
on a paved street, where hopscotching kids
paused and pointed at the sky in the direction
of the route and destination of the smoke.

Rimbaud Dying

Most days, she pins an orchid into her black hair.
Extravagant petal-crests of white and a dark trough.
Tonight, no orchid, she leans over the man in the bed
hoping he may linger and she can again collect wages,
fill a drawstring bag with gems. Each stone an ocean
of sharp starlight and an East Africa of terrible suffering.
Her small, thin hand in his remains a kindness. Mercy.

Again she offers a thin rawhide to soften his screams.
Places the strap in his mouth. It's his season in hell—
nursed by an inamorata smelling of patchouli. Proof
that comfort, unlike forgiveness, can be conscripted.
Outside, no stars. No tolling bells on midnight streets.
Only the annoying buzz of a fly that will see tomorrow.
She curses at the fly in French as a pain-cry subsides

into a string of Bedouin oaths. When he's gone, fallen
back, she traces the braille of bite marks in the leather.
The fly loots a flesh-crumb nesting in the bedclothes.
Her eyes fix on the amputation-to-the-knee as elegy.
She knows nothing of Verlaine, the trouble in Paris.
Fluent in French, she recalls the last hours and his
mad ramblings and wishes she'd worn the flower.